Please Return
to
E. W. Rowland

INSTITUTE OF PACIFIC RELATIONS

INQUIRY SERIES

THE INSTITUTE OF PACIFIC RELATIONS

The Institute of Pacific Relations is an unofficial and non-political body, founded in 1925 to facilitate the scientific study of the peoples of the Pacific Area. It is composed of National Councils in eleven countries.

The Institute as such and the National Councils of which it is composed are precluded from expressing an opinion on any aspect of national or international affairs; opinions expressed in this study are, therefore, purely individual.

NATIONAL COUNCILS OF THE INSTITUTE

American Council, Institute of Pacific Relations

Australian Institute of International Affairs

Canadian Institute of International Affairs

China Institute of Pacific Relations

Comité d'Études des Problèmes du Pacifique

Japanese Council, Institute of Pacific Relations

Netherlands-Netherlands Indies Council, Institute of Pacific Relations

New Zealand Institute of International Affairs

Philippine Council, Institute of Pacific Relations

Royal Institute of International Affairs

U.S.S.R. Council, Institute of Pacific Relations

PREREQUISITES TO PEACE IN THE FAR EAST

PREREQUISITES TO PEACE
IN THE FAR EAST

By

NATHANIEL PEFFER

Associate Professor of International Relations
Columbia University

I.P.R. INQUIRY SERIES

INTERNATIONAL SECRETARIAT
INSTITUTE OF PACIFIC RELATIONS
PUBLICATIONS OFFICE, 129 EAST 52ND STREET, NEW YORK
1940

FOREWORD

This study forms part of the documentation of an Inquiry organized by the Institute of Pacific Relations into the problems arising from the conflict in the Far East.

It has been prepared by Mr. Nathaniel Peffer, Associate Professor of International Relations, Columbia University; author of *China: The Collapse of a Civilization* (1930), and *Must We Fight in Asia?* (1935).

The study has been submitted in draft to a number of authorities, many of whom made suggestions and criticisms. In accordance with the standard policy of the Institute, however, the author was left free to accept or to reject these suggestions and criticisms. The authorities to whom this was submitted do not, of course, accept responsibility for the study. By its very nature, a study of this type must be a matter of personal interpretation and for this reason it is desirable to stress the point normally mentioned in the Foreword to this series that the statements of fact or of opinion appearing herein do not represent the view of the Institute of Pacific Relations or of the Pacific Council or of any of the National Councils. Such statements are made on the sole responsibility of the author. As was to be expected, such a study of a controversial issue has revealed a wide variety of opinion from readers and no doubt will continue to do so. Such comments will be welcomed by the Secretariat in the hope that in subsequent Inquiry studies bearing on the general problem of a Far Eastern settlement, these and other points of view can be treated. Obviously, as the author himself recognizes, there are alternative and additional approaches and interpretations which have not been included in this study.

During 1938 the Inquiry was carried on under the general direction of Dr. J. W. Dafoe as Chairman of the Pacific Council and in 1939 under his successor, Dr. Philip C. Jessup. Every member of the International Secretariat has contributed to the research and editorial work in connection with the Inquiry, but special mention should be made of Mr. W. L. Holland, Miss Kate Mitchell and Miss Hilda Austern, who have carried the major share of this responsibility. The Japanese Council has not found it possible to participate in the Inquiry, and assumes, therefore, no responsibility either for its results or for its organization.

In the general conduct of this Inquiry into the problems arising from the conflict in the Far East the Institute has benefited by the counsel of the following Advisers:

Professor H. F. Angus of the University of British Columbia
Dr. J. B. Condliffe of the University of California
M. Etienne Dennery of the Ecole des Sciences Politiques.

These advisers have co-operated with the Chairman and the Secretary-General in an effort to insure that the publications issued in connection with the Inquiry conform to a proper standard of sound and impartial scholarship. Each manuscript has been submitted to at least two of the Advisers and although they do not necessarily subscribe to the statements or views in this or any of the studies, they consider this study to be a useful contribution to the subject of the Inquiry.

The purpose of this Inquiry is to relate unofficial scholarship to the problems arising from the present situation in the Far East. Its purpose is to provide members of the Institute in all countries and the members of I.P.R. Conferences with an impartial and constructive analysis of the situation in the Far East with a view to indicating the major issues which must be considered in any future adjustment of international relations in that area. To this end, the analysis will include an account of the economic and political conditions which produced the situation existing in July 1937, with respect to China, to Japan and to the other foreign Powers concerned; an evaluation of developments during the war period which appear to indicate important trends in the policies and programs of all the Powers in relation to the Far Eastern situation; and finally, an estimate of the principal political, economic and social conditions which may be expected in a post-war period, the possible forms of adjustment which might be applied under these conditions, and the effects of such adjustments upon the countries concerned.

The Inquiry does not propose to "document" a specific plan for dealing with the Far Eastern situation. Its aim is to focus available information on the present crisis in forms which will be useful to those who lack either the time or the expert knowledge to study the vast amount of material now appearing or already published in a number of languages. Attention may also be drawn to a series of studies on topics bearing on the Far Eastern situation which is being prepared by the Japanese Council. That series is being undertaken entirely independently of this Inquiry, and for its organization and publication the Japanese Council alone is responsible.

The present study, "Prerequisites to Peace in the Far East," is one of several which will fall within the framework of the last of the four general groups of studies which it is proposed to make as follows:

I. The political and economic conditions which have contributed to the present course of the policies of Western Powers in the Far East; their territorial and economic interests; the effects on their Far

Eastern policies of internal economic and political developments and of developments in their foreign policies vis-à-vis other parts of the world; the probable effects of the present conflict on their positions in the Far East; their changing attitudes and policies with respect to their future relations in that area.

II. The political and economic conditions which have contributed to the present course of Japanese foreign policy and possible important future developments; the extent to which Japan's policy toward China has been influenced by Japan's geographic conditions and material resources, by special features in the political and economic organization of Japan which directly or indirectly affect the formulation of her present foreign policy, by economic and political developments in China, by the external policies of other Powers affecting Japan; the principal political, economic and social factors which may be expected in a post-war Japan; possible and probable adjustments on the part of other nations which could aid in the solution of Japan's fundamental problems.

III. The political and economic conditions which have contributed to the present course of Chinese foreign policy and possible important future developments; Chinese unification and reconstruction, 1931-37, and steps leading toward the policy of united national resistance to Japan; the present degree of political cohesion and economic strength; effects of resistance and current developments on the position of foreign interests in China and changes in China's relations with foreign Powers; the principal political, economic and social factors which may be expected in a post-war China; possible and probable adjustments on the part of other nations which could aid in the solution of China's fundamental problems.

IV. Possible methods for the adjustment of specific problems, in the light of information and suggestions presented in the three studies outlined above; analysis of previous attempts at bilateral or multilateral adjustments of political and economic relations in the Pacific and causes of their success or failure; types of administrative procedures and controls already tried out and their relative effectiveness; the major issues likely to require international adjustment in a post-war period and the most hopeful methods which might be devised to meet them; necessary adjustments by the Powers concerned; the basic requirements of a practical system of international organization which could promote the security and peaceful development of the countries of the Pacific area.

EDWARD C. CARTER
Secretary-General

New York,
October 8, 1940

CONTENTS

FOREWORD vii

I. THE PROBLEM STATED 3

II. FAR EASTERN CONFLICT IN THE MAKING . 11

III. AT STAKE IN THE CONFLICT 35

IV. CONDITIONS TO LASTING PEACE 62

V. JAPAN'S LEGITIMATE NEEDS 75

VI. THE INTERNAL NEEDS OF CHINA . . . 98

POSTSCRIPT 114

xi

PREREQUISITES TO PEACE IN THE FAR EAST

CHAPTER I

THE PROBLEM STATED

The purpose of this study is simply stated. It is to ask what are the bases of a durable peace in the Far East. The question has regard not only to the war now in progress between China and Japan but to the larger conflict out of which this war arose, out of which others have arisen before and in which every great country is involved, though at one remove. Thus seen, the question is rather: what settlement of the war now in progress will preclude its recurrence out of the same causes? Or, in the larger sense, how can there be prevented in the Far East a repetition in the next generation of that which we have seen in Europe in this generation—a catastrophic war, a peace settlement that leaves all the causes of war in operation and lays the ground for future conflict, and then a resumption of the conflict on exactly the same grounds as before?

As this is written, China and Japan have been at war for more than three years. When or how the war will end no one can say. Probably it will not end at all in the sense that on a certain day one can say: today peace has been restored in the Far East. In that sense modern wars do not end, as contemporary Europe testifies. Wars cannot be conclusive when they represent struggles not of armies but of whole peoples, of economies, of societies. There can only be a decisive superiority established on the battlefield, signalized by a truce called a treaty of peace and then followed by a lull in which conflict is transferred to another medium, while physical forces are marshalled for a renewed trial at arms. So it has been in Europe for more than twenty years, and so it doubtless will be in the Far East, no matter what the outcome of the fighting in the interior of China.

In the Far East it is peculiarly unlikely that there can be a conclusive decision by force of arms. On the one hand, there is the disparity of area and population in China's favor, on the other hand the disparity in technological proficiency and social organization in Japan's favor. The two cancel each other out for purposes of genuine conquest. China could not acquire an ascendancy over Japan even if it would, for Japan is unreachably superior in military power; Japan could not maintain the lasting ascendancy over China that it seeks, for China is spread over half a continent, has a population five times as large as Japan's and has acquired a consciousness of national identity. There can be a military victory—a Japanese military victory, that is to say—but it would be official only. It would constitute a pause, marked by continued informal resistance and recurrent outbreaks on a large scale—war in successive though intermittent phases.

It is not unfitting then to discuss the underlying issues in the Far East and their settlement without regard to what the military result of the war may be or when it comes or even if it should come before these pages appear. For they cannot be settled or even fundamentally affected by fighting, by technical decisions registered on the battlefield, by "imposing the will on the enemy." The Japanese may force the Chinese to

surrender; but all they will have then is the right to
dictate the peace treaty, to formulate the conditions of
the relationship between China and Japan in the near
future or, in other words, to write down the terms of a
truce. This might be enough to throw added weights in
one scale in the balance of world politics at a critical
moment, but it would not offer a solution to China
and Japan or therefore to the larger problems of international relations affecting the whole world. The
basic conflict in the Far East, involving China and
Japan in the first instance and the rest of the world at
one remove, would remain to give rise no doubt to
future wars. With that conflict this study is concerned,
its purpose being to analyze the constituent elements
of the conflict and to ask what instead would constitute
the elements of a lasting peace in the Far East.

If it can be assumed that there is some freedom of
will in international relations and that conscious power
can be exercised to eliminate the disorders that preclude any arbitrament but force, what measures can be
taken to prevent the recurrence of the kind of struggle
that is now devastating a large part of a continent, ruin-
ing the lives of tens of millions and threatening to draw
the rest of the world into its vortex? What settlement
will conduce to the establishment of an international
political and social equilibrium in the Far East that will
enable Far Eastern nations to live in peace, absolve
Occidental nations from the danger of being involved
in wars on the other side of the world and assure to all
nations fair access to the riches of the Far East without
impinging on the independence, security and welfare
of Far Eastern peoples? After this war or after some

future war these questions will have to be faced. As-suming that after this war the situation not only in the Far East but elsewhere in the world makes it possible to deal with them now, what are the facts and considerations that bear on them? That is the subject of this inquiry.

Such an inquiry is appropriate at this time. Europe, too, is at war. Regardless of where victory lies, one international system has ended and another is to begin. It is clear now that the hopes with which the war began are not to be fulfilled. The thoughts of men everywhere were occupied with enterprises of refashioning the world on a new principle of order in the peace settlement. But those hopes and projects were conditional on a decisive Anglo-French victory, more especially on an Anglo-French victory consummated before the destruction of a prolonged war generated passions that swept away all except desire for revenge. They are now abortive hopes and projects. Nevertheless it can be said with confidence (perhaps nothing else can be said with confidence as this is written, in the latter part of July, 1940) that the Western world as it stood on May 1, 1940, is no more. The post-1918 European system has been disestablished. It may be more accurate to say that the post-Napoleonic European system has been disestablished. Something else has to take its place, for the ground has been cleared. It may be only a redistribution of power in larger units—a system of giant blocs, the main components being Germany, the U.S.S.R., the United States and the victor in the Far East, each with its satellites. But whatever succeeds, relationships within the Occident and the Far East have to be restated. This will be all the more true in that the post-1918 system in the Far East, or, rather, the post-1842 system in the Far East also will have been disestablished by the China-Japan war and will have to be restated, not only in light of the results of that war but in light of the results of the European war. In fact, equilibrium will be difficult to establish and maintain in either hemisphere except in terms of the other.

No elaborate argument is necessary to demonstrate the last point. It is supported by a preponderance of historical evidence. The events of the last few years are eloquent. For nearly a hundred years the Far East has been pendant to European high politics. Sometimes directly, sometimes indirectly, the course of Far Eastern politics has been responsive to the movement of the European balance of power. Never so clearly a pawn as, say, the Balkans, the Far East has nevertheless been a token in major European manipulations and transactions. The so-called Battle of the Concessions in China at the close of the nineteenth century was a direct expression of European international relations. It was not so much the intrinsic value of the concessions wrested from China that was responsible for the infringements on China's sovereignty and territorial integrity as the desire to offset gains made by European rivals. One European state acquired a leasehold on Chinese soil or a special position or right in China's administrative service; every other state had to get an equivalent in kind to counterbalance the increase in political power and the enhancement of prestige. The Anglo-Japanese alliance, the effects of which are still being felt, was similarly a reflection of balance of power considerations—the need of a counter-check to Russia. It may even be said that China's continued existence as a nation to this day can be attributed in the main to the state of European rivalries. It is one of the legends of American historical writing that America prevented the partition of China during and after the Boxer Rebellion; the fact is rather that China escaped partition because European rivalries and jealousies obviated an agreement on the division of the spoils, and the balance of power, already struck though not yet fixed, prevented any one party from taking the initiative to appropriate to itself all of China or its most valuable parts.

Japan owes its rapid elevation to the rank of great Power not so much to its own efforts as to the consequences of the first World War. Both economically and politically that war gave Japan its opportunity. Without that opportunity Japan would not have been able until much later to arrive at the position from which it could challenge for ascendancy over China. It was the gathering crisis in Europe, with the Italian threat in the Mediterranean and the advent of the Nazi regime, that enabled Japan to proceed, at least with the appearance of impunity, to attempt to consummate the conquest of China. The conclusion of the Japanese-German anti-Comintern pact so-called gave Japan the presumptive security to embark on the war in 1937; without European complications that pact would not have conferred even the appearance of such security. And since 1937 it is scarcely likely that Great Britain, France and the United States would have remained inert in the face of the infringement of their political and economic rights in the Far East had it not been for the imminence of the European war.

Finally, now that the European war has come, it need not be said that thereby the fate of Far Eastern territories is being determined no less than that of Europe. A victory for Germany, with or without the adherence of the U.S.S.R. and Italy, would mean the dissolution of the British, French and Dutch empires in the Far East. The inheritance would be determined according to the relations between the victors in the two hemispheres or, it might be, according to the decisions taken by America as to the risks warranted by the desire to maintain the status quo in the Pacific and adjacent waters. At any event it is clear that the future of the Far East is being played out in Europe as well as the Far East, and equally clear that until the final disposition is made of Eastern territories it is hardly likely that Europe can return to a state of security and poise. While a redistribution of power is in process in the Far East, Europe or certain states in Europe will remain on guard to ensure a distribution they deem fair.

It is no longer possible to separate East and West in the politics of war and peace. If Europe could compose its internecine feuds and succeed in establishing a new international order in the West, it would still have no immunity from war until there was some assurance of peace in the East. The war between China and Japan, coming at the same time as the European conflict, may usher in a new succession of wars for imperial power, collateral perhaps with wars of social doctrine, wars expanded to embrace continents; or it may be ended with a peace that extricates the Far East from the arena of recurrent conflict for imperial power and by so much helps the Western nations to exempt themselves from the necessity of war for stakes that are remote, however valuable in terms of power and economic gain. A German victory or the victory of a fascist bloc headed by Germany does not alter the principles which underlie settlement in the Far East. It may make their application impossible now or change the method of their application; but it does not invalidate them. For solution now or later, the problem remains: how can peace in the Far East be contrived, peace within the Far East and between the Far East and the Western world?

CHAPTER II

FAR EASTERN CONFLICT IN THE MAKING

What is the Far Eastern conflict? In the Far East as in any other international setting the present can be understood only in terms of the past, and any effort to deal intelligently with the future is conditional on a grasp of both present and past. Like any other war, the war that began in 1937 was the result of more than the events which immediately preceded it. The conflict in the Far East has a long lineage, not so long perhaps as the European conflict and having fewer collateral lines but of the same order. The war between China and Japan was inevitable: not in the sense of preordination or fate or the scheme of things but in the sense of the operation of cause and effect. It had to come, because almost every event in the Far East of international import for the last hundred years had gone into its making, because almost every act of the great Powers involved in the Far East had contributed to that end. The causes of the war may be grouped in two categories: the long-range causes working cumulatively since the middle of the nineteenth century and the recent controversies between China and Japan directly, culminating in a minor skirmish near Peiping in July, 1937. Of these the long-range causes are the more important, since they created the atmosphere which endowed the controversies with more than their intrinsic value and made it easy for a skirmish to expand into a full-fledged war. And the whole Far Eastern problem

11

cannot be understood or the Far Eastern conflict settled unless seen as an historical continuity.

There is no need here to give any detailed history of Far Eastern international relations or of the foreign encroachments on Chinese soil which are their chief content. That has been treated in numerous standard works. It is sufficient to mark the main stages in the course that has led to the present tragic pass. It has been a course with occasional divagations but proceeding always in the same direction. Given the direction fixed, there could have been no other destination than that at which the Far East has arrived. Fifty years ago Japan's present attempt to conquer China might have been foreseen as a projection of what had already been set in motion. Japan's attempt has unique properties and characteristics, deriving from the peculiar nature of the Japanese state and society, the peculiar qualities of a dominant feudal military caste having at its disposal the powerful instruments of modern industrialism; but it is of the same order as that which preceded it.

The stages almost mark themselves. First was the period of the breaking down of China's seclusion and the forcible entry of the principal Western Powers by means of two wars, the first concluded by the peace of 1842 and the second by the peace of 1860. The disintegration of China then began, accelerating as the century wore to its close, and by the last two decades China's truncation was in process, each Power taking what it could in proportion to its military strength. With loss of territory, foreign concessions and settlements on its soil and foreign control of important parts of its administration, China had for all practical purposes lost its sovereignty. It was laid in subjection to what can be called a collective master—reduced but not yet divided. It was China's good fortune and perhaps the ill fortune of the rest of the world that no single Western country was strong enough to make itself exclusive master of China and thus end the struggle for control. England came nearest, and in the Far East as elsewhere since the middle of the nineteenth century there were tragic consequences from the fact that England came near enough to supremacy to arouse jealousy, envy and hostility but not so near that challenge could not be given with impunity. China was thus held in a kind of international diplomatic escrow, to be disposed of after a final settlement among the great Powers by arbitrament of arms.

In the meantime there was the familiar combination of diplomatic intrigue, manipulation, maneuvering, threat and counter-threat, move and counter-move— the traditional preliminaries to war. Each great Power strove to displace every other Power in China and to win priority for itself. China became progressively more helpless, more clearly an inanimate counter in a game of world politics. The Far East became a pendant to the European balance of power, shifting as it shifted; in the twenty years preceding the first World War the state of European politics could have been read at any time in the state of affairs in the Far East. On China's part there were occasional desperate attempts at self-assertion and salvation, the most conspicuous being the Boxer uprising in 1900; but more and more it subsided into fatalistic resignation. Occasional efforts were made by certain Powers to postpone or obviate partition. One instance was the enunciation of the Open Door policy by the United States in 1899. Another was Japan's war against Russia to impede the glacial Russian movement over Manchuria and North China, a war which resulted only in Japan's supplanting Russia in the role of aspirant to dominion by conquest. But these were either half-hearted, ineffectual or dictated by dog-in-the-manger considerations. As the nineteenth century passed into the twentieth China's extinction appeared to be certain. There appeared to be in question only when it would be consummated and to which nation would accrue political power over China and the profit from its economic exploitation.

The World War intervened. The struggle in the Far East was suspended pending decision in Europe and China won a reprieve. But in the Far East as elsewhere the status quo ante was never restored and could not be restored. In the Far East as elsewhere all the forces in operation before 1914 were given new direction, if not new content. The war injected two new elements into the Far East. In the first place, it gave a new focal point to the struggle for mastery over China. The center moved eastward. On Japan was conferred a free hand by the preoccupation in Europe of the Western Powers that had hitherto been the main contenders. Japan made an effort in 1915 through the Twenty-one Demands to establish what would have been in effect a protectorate over China, but the effort was abortive, balked by a combination of China's firmness and the opposition of the Western Powers. For one thing Japan did not yet feel secure enough overtly to defy the West. Though abortive at first, the effort was never to be relaxed, but instead was to be prosecuted with increasing vigor until it precipitated the war in 1937. From 1914 onward the pace was forced by Japan and the Western Powers lagged ever further behind. Simultaneously internal dissensions in China, resulting from the breakdown in the traditional political system of which the revolution of 1911 was symptom rather than cause, further weakened China's power of resistance. The question then became not so much which of the great Powers would acquire hegemony over China as whether or not Japan would do so. But consummation no longer appeared to be certain, as it had before 1914. For the second new element injected by the World War was a change in China. China ceased to be inanimate and subsident, and therewith the Far East entered upon the second stage.

Historians may write one day that the effects of the first World War were no less deep and lasting in the East than in the West, where it was fought. For throughout the East the war gave a tremendous impetus to currents of native nationalism. These had their source in the times, to be sure, and would have arisen in any circumstances, but without the war they would not have had the force they acquired in the post-war decade and that decade might have been different. What would have been a slow gathering process was telescoped into a few years. The reasons are easy to discern. The wide diffusion of the Wilsonian body of ideas, with their emphasis on the rights of small nations and international justice, was enough in itself. It awoke national consciousness where none had existed before and sharpened such as already existed. The appeal of both sides in the war to their colonies, protectorates and other dependencies to offer help generated in the subject peoples a sense of their own worth and, what is more, a recognition of their potential power—a power that could be used in their own interests as well as in the interests of their alien masters. The abusive propaganda of both sides undermined what was known as the white man's prestige, and on this even more than on armed might rested the rule of the empires. Furthermore, both sides, the Allies in particular, brought soldiers of the subject races to the fighting fronts and there used them to kill white men. This lesson, too, they were to recognize as one that could be applied in their own interests. The whole system of values which was the foundation of the white empires was shaken. And when it became manifest that the empires had been depleted in military strength by the war, the desire for independence born of the new-found or accentuated nationalism coincided with the conviction that it might be won, and the two soon led to the succession of colonial uprisings that characterized the decade after the war. Regardless of the extent to which these were successful, the relations between the empires were never again to be the same. The dependencies themselves were never again to be the same. The simplicities of nineteenth century two-dimensional politics were no more. Henceforth there was to be rivalry among empires as in the nineteenth century and at the same time struggle, overt or latent, between the empires and their dependencies to determine whether the dependencies were to remain in subjection or become free.

Of no other part of the world was this so conspicuously true as of China. There had been a nascent nationalism in China since the revolution which overthrew the alien dynasty of the Manchus in 1911. China had been taken into the war as an associate of the Allies and then betrayed at the peace conference, when the former German possessions on Chinese soil were awarded to Japan rather than retroceded to China. From that point the nascent nationalism was to attain rapid growth and to become aggressive. Indeed, it may be said that at that point it became certain that a war would have to be fought between China and one great Power or another unless China was to be given independence by voluntary cession, that is, all concessions and settlements retroceded and all special privileges in derogation of China's sovereignty nullified. In other words, some Power would have to do what Japan is now attempting to do.

The turn events were to take was soon foreshadowed. The shock of the settlement at Versailles released something long pent up in China. There were newly formed patriotic associations, student movements, mass demonstrations, general strikes and outbursts of violence. What came to be called the unequal treaties, the agreements made under duress by which foreign nations had acquired rights contravening Chinese sovereignty, became a symbol and rallying-cry. However disunited China was to remain internally, in its external relations at least the educated classes were to find common ground—the resolve to free the country from alien in-

fringements. This ground has never been seriously
shaken. It underlies the present war.

Rumblings in the East became audible in the West,
rumblings of alien discontent and of the first clash of
renewed international rivalries. They fell on ears still
sensitive from the alarums of European war, and in
cognizance of the warnings the Washington Conference
was convoked in 1921, with the double purpose of
limiting naval armaments and examining questions
susceptible of international conflict in the Far East. In
its first purpose the conference was successful. It
brought about a standstill in naval construction for ten
years, thus alleviating some international strains and
obviating those that might arise from a naval race. In
its second purpose the conference had meager results,
notwithstanding the amplitude of rhetorical pronouncements. Pledges of self-restraint were made in
vague generalities—pledges of the kind that were being
made throughout the period of the spoliation of China.
The Powers bound themselves not to steal a march on
each other in China—bonds of the kind that have the
most delicate fragility in intercourse among great
Powers. But as between the great Powers on the one
hand and China on the other everything was left essentially unchanged. China formally asked restitution
of its sovereign rights—tariff autonomy, abolition of
extraterritoriality, retrocession of foreign territorial
possessions or leaseholds on its soil, among other things.
In response the Powers agreed to close the post of-
fices they maintained in China, and for the rest ad-
jured China to set its house in order and some day
in the future—not defined—it would be deemed—by

criteria not specified—to be worthy of exercising the rights of an independent nation. In a word, the Powers kept all that they had in China. Their position vis-à-vis China was unchanged; their position vis-à-vis each other was unchanged. China was still subject to foreign encroachment and supervision, if not control; the Powers were still in the relationship of rivalry for predominance over China. If rivalry for possession or domination of rich but weak lands is among the causes of war, then China remained a war arena.

The Washington Conference was negative in accomplishment but positive in result. Its acts of omission had effects as weighty and direct as if they had been acts of commission, though in a different direction. They gave fresh stimulus to Chinese nationalism. The Chinese had been denied satisfaction under circumstances that made the denial not only a rebuff but a challenge. Washington was different from Versailles. At Versailles the Far East was a side issue and the press of more exigent problems could be offered as excuse for its cursory consideration, which could be construed as inaction rather than unfavorable action. But Washington was concerned with the Far East alone. The issue was unclouded and unmixed. Inaction constituted rebuff. The Chinese had come to Washington with hopes that their demands would be met at least in part. When the demands were refused and hopes dashed, the effect was worse than if the occasion for hope had never arisen. A goad was sharpened. In China there was disappointment, then a gathering resolve to put no more hopes in requests or demands but to resort to action.

Whatever may be credited to the Washington Conference for its obviation of a naval race, in its political
aspects it was unfortunate. It hastened a dangerous
climax in the Far East. Certain forces had already been
set in motion that could not have been arrested in any
event. They were in the time, created and formed by
the ideas of an historical period. But their mass and
velocity could have been lessened, their impact on the
world politics of a generation already sorely beset
might have been cushioned. Nothing could have prevented the Chinese, in common with other nations
that had been subjected by strong empires in the century of Western conquests, from seeking to recover
their independence. Given nationalism as the ruling
principle of group organization since the end of the
eighteenth century and the development of communications throughout the nineteenth century to dissemi-
nate the principle, no human power could have prevented the Chinese from coming under the influence
of nationalism and pursuing the aspirations it generated. In other words, no human power could have
kept the Chinese content with their quasi-colonial
status. Under any circumstances the first half of the
twentieth century was to see the growth and resolution
of conflict in the Far East, a conflict turning on
whether China was to recover independence or the
empires were to retain the privileges which derogated
from Chinese sovereignty. But the conflict might have
been resolved in stages, graduated to ease the necessary
political and economic adjustments, each stage taken
without emotional tensions. To that end concessions
were required—concessions liberal enough to prevent

the growth of intransigence and yet not so costly as to entail any serious sacrifice to the great Powers. Most of all, they had to be made in time.

There is a time factor in international relations. It is perhaps the major factor. What is done is no more important than when it is done. Measures effective at one time may be futile at another time. Concessions made on request can work for conciliation; concessions made on demand, after feelings have been exacerbated and irreversible positions taken, usually only serve as incitations to larger demands, for they are construed as signs of weakness. Then still greater concessions are required, concessions that cannot or will not be made; but if they are not made, waves of resentment gather that sweep over attempts to weigh rationally the intrinsic merits of the issues between the nations in controversy. Then compromise is no longer possible. By way of example there is Germany in the West or China in the East. In the East the crucial time was the period just following the World War, when the influences released by the war were only beginning to flow and Oriental nationalism had not yet gathered momentum. The Washington Conference offered the opportunity. The opportunity was missed. It may very well have been the last opportunity. The concessions were not made. The waves of resentment gathered on the horizon.

The forces that already had been set in motion in the Far East were accelerated, then, rather than impeded by such action as the nations principally concerned took or failed to take. At the best they would have marched to a dangerous juncture. As it turned

out, they derived additional momentum from an extraneous dynamic—the intervention of Soviet Russia
through the Communist International. That chapter
of Far Eastern history also has been told too often to
need detailed recounting here. In brief, an alliance was
contracted between the Kuomintang, or Chinese Nationalist party, and Soviet Russia. They were drawn
together by needs that were complementary, if not
common, both of them being in a sense disinherited.

The Kuomintang had been the party of national lib-
eration since its founding by the enigmatic Sun Yat-
sen. It had freed the country from the yoke of the alien
Manchu dynasty, and the mission of freeing the
country from the yoke of foreign imperialism fell on
it naturally. At the same time it was a party in opposition, just then at its lowest ebb, even under a kind of
proscription by the military cabals then ruling the
country. Nationalism, anti-imperialism, anti-foreignism and independence were the wheels of a vehicle on
which it could ride back into popular favor.

Soviet Russia for its part also was proscribed and
had worked itself into a blind alley. The Communist
International found itself compelled to abandon the
hope of an early world revolution radiating from
Russia through Europe and America. The capitalist
system in the Occident was not breaking down according to the schedule set by communist prognosis, nor
was there any sign of imminent breakdown. The system as it stood in the West was stronger than the communist theoreticians had confidently calculated. If the
capitalistic nations and thereby the system were to be
successfully attacked, their weak points had to be

found elsewhere. These lay, to all appearances, on the peripheries of the great empires, which were also the strongholds of the capitalistic system.

In fact, capitalism *was* imperialism and once imperialism was undone capitalism would cease to be. The rumblings of colonial disaffection, of native nationalism, were evidence in corroboration of theory and plainly laid the course of action. There the weak points were, and on the first principles of political as well as military strategy there the attack was to be delivered. The most promising area was China; there the empires themselves had prepared the ground.

The agreement between the Kuomintang and Soviet Russia was concluded in 1923. It was an agreement in generalities which could be translated into a pledge of mutual support. The Russians gave their pledge tangible form in short order by sending political and military "advisers." Under the guidance of these advisers the Kuomintang underwent an internal revolution. From a loose association of men of liberal inclinations, politically rather than socially liberal, it became a militant, highly organized body, more or less on the pattern of the Soviet party system. Its program as publicly avowed emphasized the political aspects rather than the social. It was still a nationalistic party, dedicated to freeing the country from the trammels of imperialism, rather than a party of social revolution. In fact, the original Soviet-Chinese agreement explicitly repudiated any intention of instituting a communist or even soviet system in China. Internal conditions were unsuited to such a system, it was admitted.

With nationalism as its appeal and Russian guidance

in organization and propaganda to give the appeal the widest diffusion and highest effectiveness, the Kuomintang went forward, and with every stride in advance it gained fresh access of strength. At the same time it was acquiring military power, for it had a cause with which to win recruits and hold them and it had expert assistance in making a proficient modern army of them. The opposition to it was negative, without a cause and without real power. The warring military satraps who had been misruling the country had antagonized the people, and their military strength was in façade only, effective when facing others of their ilk. They were swept away by the more disciplined soldiers of the Nationalists, fighting for ends they could understand and with the support of a sympathetic populace.

As the Nationalists gained adherents through their propaganda and territory through the victories of their troops, their program crystallized in content and sharpened in vigor. Popularly expressed in the slogan "Down with Imperialism," it was translated as policy into outright abolition of foreign territorial possessions and cancellation of foreign special positions and administrative controls. It meant the eviction of the foreigners except as resident alien traders subject to Chinese law. The prospect of success was becoming more auspicious as the Nationalists swept up through the country in 1925 and 1926 from their base in Canton. Enthusiasm mounted throughout the country, internal opposition was melting away, and the foreign Powers were helpless, for they were left too depleted by the World War for military expeditions to another hemisphere and their people were in no mood for military adventurings.

A climax appeared to be approaching early in 1927 when the British were forced to surrender their concession in Hankow after it had been overrun by a mob with Nationalistic troops behind them. The climax would doubtless have come, had there not intervened another conflict, a conflict produced by the inherent contradiction in the Kuomintang-Soviet alliance itself. For the motive of the preponderant element of the Kuomintang's leaders was nationalism—recovery of national independence. The motive of the Russians was the formation of an attack on the imperialistic flank of capitalism. While assisting the Kuomintang to get control of the country in order to eject the foreigners the Russians were boring from within to get control of the Kuomintang. While the Chinese leaders of the Kuomintang were making political revolution, the Chinese communists under the tutelage of the Russians were laying the ground for social revolution. The popular slogans were being broadened from dispossession of foreign imperialism to dispossession of Chinese wealth. As amended, they were even more infectious in a country predominantly dwelling in poverty which was degraded even according to pre-industrial standards. The communists were utopian in promise of material blessings, and by comparison national sovereignty was a remote and tenuous concept. The issue came to a head in 1927. Either the nationalist, non-communist leaders of the Kuomintang had to abdicate to the communists and by corollary the country became an annex of the Third International or the communists had to be expelled. The communists were expelled, under circumstances that need not be discussed here but that reflected no credit on either side. Among the uglier accompaniments was a white terror prosecuted with horrors excessive even to the genre.

The Russian advisers were expelled and the Chinese communists killed or driven under cover, but the pressure on foreign interests was unrelaxed. To the contrary, it was intensified in proportion as the foreign Powers failed to take retaliation, either out of unwillingness or inability. It was time to capitalize their weakness; the Chinese raised their demands. The Nationalists occupied Peking, then the capital, and became the de facto government. In full control, they were then in a position officially to treat with the foreign Powers, but now as claimants and not as supplicants. The 1842-1922 phase of Far Eastern history had closed. And in the negotiations that followed through 1928 the Chinese exacted several times more than they would have been happy to receive six years earlier. Conversely, had the Powers granted willingly in 1922 half as much as they found themselves compelled to yield in 1928, they would have won gratitude and saved the balance for much longer than six years. From every indication at the time the passing of all foreign rights and interests in China was under way and would have been consummated, had it not been that the rift opened by the expulsion of the communists widened. The newly cemented unity was shattered. The spirit of dedication was dulled. There was a reversion to warlord government, and the public morale sank. A respite was given the foreign Powers in the sense that they were no longer compelled to stand and deliver; but nationalist China, even with unity lost and zeal dimmed, did not remit its demands and its pressure. It had been carried too far on the wave of success to recede. In fact, not recognizing how much had been lost through schism and disenchantment, not perceiving that striking power had gone with union and enthusiasm, the Nationalists continued as exigent as they had been when they had the whole country behind them. They moved as if to make a clean sweep of foreign interests forthwith.

Had they confined themselves to the interests of Western nations, it may be that they would have succeeded, even with their striking power impaired by internal developments. For the Western governments were neither in the position nor in the mood to retort with force. But the Chinese did not confine themselves to Western interests. They were too carried away by their first successes to make calm appraisals of strength. They attributed those successes not to the temporary weakness of the Western Powers but to their own strength, an error that begot overconfidence and consequences fatal to themselves. It led them to challenge all foreign Powers, forgetting that there were Powers that were not hampered by distance, by war-weariness or by the necessity of paying heed to public opinion. In short, they ignored the fact that Soviet Russia and Japan also were interested parties and were not under the same handicaps, politically and geographically, as Europe and the United States. But any attack on foreign interests as such struck at Russia and Japan equally with Europe and America. For Soviet Russia had con-

trol of the Chinese Eastern Railway and at least a voice
in North Manchuria, while Japan had substantive
control of the South Manchuria Railway and effective
control of South Manchuria. Full recovery of lost territory and sovereign rights would not only negate such
imperial pretensions as those two Powers had but
undermine their imperial positions. And the Chinese
proceeded toward such recovery, not so much con-
temptuous of caution as oblivious to its necessity. They
were both over-estimating their own strength and
under-estimating the strength of their opposition. It
was China's most vital mistake in the last generation.
It may prove to have been a fatal mistake. But the
possibility of such a mistake would not have existed
had it not been for the Russian alliance and the too
easy successes it begot, with the deceptive appearance
of strength thus conveyed.

China did give the challenge, both to Soviet Russia
and to Japan. In 1929 the Chinese regional government in Manchuria seized the Chinese Eastern Railway, a survival of Tsarist imperialism which Communist Russia had not relinquished, and arrested the
Russian officials in charge. Soviet Russia took swift
and drastic retaliation. An expedition drove into Manchuria, put the ill-trained Chinese troops to flight and
forced China to a humiliating surrender. It is a
piquant commentary on the politics of these years that
reversion to the orthodox practice of punitive expeditions in the Far East was initiated by Soviet Russia,
defender of oppressed nations and classes. The incident
served as a warning to Japan and as a temptation. It
was indication that China was disposed to resort to

direct action to recover its rights and also that China could be disposed of easily by any country willing to put forth the required military power.

Throughout the period from 1923 to 1927 Japan had remained passive. A relatively liberal group had wielded governmental power during those years. The ideas released by the World War had penetrated Japan, too. In 1928 a more aggressive group of the familiar Japanese military pattern returned to power. It was not passive by temperament or conviction, and it had already been chafing from a succession of events in Manchuria, where the Chinese regional regime had declared its adhesion to the Nationalist government at Nanking despite Japanese prohibition. There were more compelling causes for restiveness. As part of the general revitalization in those years China had begun to push forward its reconstruction by modernization, and this had been extended to South Manchuria. China had begun to build railways in Manchuria, including some that paralleled the Japanese-controlled South Manchuria Railway, and Chinese capital was setting up industrial, financial and mercantile enterprises in direct competition with the Japanese. There were signs that if the process was not checked, Japan would soon be exercising the formalities of political control in Manchuria while China would be extracting the material benefits. This, combined with China's general air of defiance, was a goad to the Japanese army in Manchuria, a group hardly given to turning the other cheek. There was mounting tension and a succession of minor incidents. In the night of September 18-19, 1931, occurred the most serious incident, perhaps being contrived by the Japanese themselves, and there began what ended in the conquest of all Manchuria, the establishment of Manchukuo, and the last stage in the development of the Far Eastern tragedy. The history of that episode and its aftermath, with the European complications, the failure of the League of Nations and the Washington Government and the repercussions therefrom on the course of European events, is too familiar to need detailing.

So far as the Far East itself is concerned, Japan had assumed the aggressive and has never since relinquished it. Beginning with what may be called a defensive effort to retain its hold on South Manchuria against the claims of Chinese nationalism, Japan pressed forward in an attempt to extend its grasp on North Manchuria, Inner Mongolia and North China. In 1932 came the attack on Shanghai. In the next year came the attack on Jehol and North China inside the Great Wall. In 1935 began the overt attempt to detach the North China provinces from China proper and form them into a so-called autonomous regime under Japanese aegis. It failed in its full purpose, but China had to compromise to the extent of permitting the formation of a so-called North China Political Council, under Japanese veto if not supervision. At the same time there was set up a separate regime in Eastern Hopei Province, which was wholly a Japanese puppet regime.

Up to this time China was compliant, too stunned to offer resistance or even hope to stem the Japanese tide. But when the full import of Japan's purposes became evident and China seemed about to come under the heel of the Japanese army, the Chinese suddenly hardened into resolve, as always when China is in what appears to be extremity. There was widespread public clamor for resistance. There was demand for cessation of surrender or compromise, for internal unification against the external enemy. The country began to arm for what was recognized to be the imminent necessity of defense in a struggle for self-preservation. From that point compromise and surrender did cease, there was progress toward unification, there was progress in armament. The Japanese advance by threat was stopped. No more was to be conceded unless Japan wrested it by force. The choice was thereafter to be Japan's.

Japan chose as the world knows. Perhaps it had already been carried so far that it could not choose otherwise. It was suffering from the disability laid on any nation that has imposed itself on another by force. It cannot make concessions either out of wisdom or out of a sense of fairness. The Japanese did not want a war. All except the most headstrong among the military leaders would have preferred a peaceful settlement, even if it had entailed a pause in Japan's continental advance. But by 1937 settlement would have entailed something more positive than pause. China was aroused. It could have been calmed again only by a token of some worth. Japan might have bought compromise and peace by cancelling the palpably bogus East Hopei regime, for example; this would have been a small price, since that regime had proved of dubious worth to Japan either politically or economically. But doing so would have signified more on Japan's part than a desire for compromise and peace. Even the least intransigent of the Japanese civilians feared that it would be construed by China as a sign of weakness and that China would proceed to capitalize the opportunity by seeking to overthrow the Japanese regime in Manchukuo. And it is quite likely that China actually would have proceeded to do so. It undoubtedly would have construed Japan's concession as a sign of fear. As has been said, Japan was suffering from the disability that lies on those that rule by the sword. It could not be reasonable even to save itself from paying a price out of all proportion to what it could gain from being adamant. Whether the ruling groups in Japan even wanted to be reasonable is uncertain. At any rate they were not. The course of events in the Far East moved with a kind of fatality. The question was only what act would precipitate the catastrophe. It came on the night of July 7 in a small clash near Peiping, and the war which was to change the history of the Eastern hemisphere was on.

These, then, are the stages in the development of the Far East from the middle of the nineteenth century to the present. They can also be called the stages in the progression of the nineteenth century into the twentieth, for each of them is an expression of the forces running in society at the time. Not much imaginative effort would be required to reconstruct from the history of the Far East since 1850 the social and economic history of the Western world for the same period.

First came the period of Western encroachment on China, and this was only a part of the larger expansive movement of the West in the nineteenth century, a movement that derived its dynamic force from the in-

dustrialization of production in the West. An industrializing society might have changed the manner of
expansion but not foregone the necessity therefor.
Then came the period of inter-imperial rivalry for
paramountcy in the Far East, and this too was integral
to a time when nationalism was the principle of order
and the reward of national expansion was economic
gain as well as glory. Then came the emergence of
Japan into competition with the Western empires for
paramountcy in the Far East, this also being inescapable when the greater facility of communication made
for the easy transmission both of ideas and technical
knowledge, thus endowing Japan with nationalism, the
capacity to produce cheaply and efficiently by machinery and the motives for expansion arising therefrom.
Then came the surge of nationalism in China, again a
phenomenon common to all subject peoples at the
time, a consequence of the communication of ideas and
thus a product of the time, being accelerated by the
World War and encouraged to effort by the weaken-
ing of the empires in that war. Then came Russian
intervention to give Chinese nationalism a power and
drive that it would not otherwise have had till much
later; nor can this be called adventitious. The social
conflict was inherent in the time. Not only by Hegelian
antithesis had Marxism arisen to challenge capitalism
as the principle of social organization. Furthermore,
Great Britain was at once the most powerful empire
and foremost protagonist of the old order and Soviet
Russia was the protagonist of the alternative. The peculiar inflection which Russian communism gave to
Marxism lent a special character to the social challenge, and perhaps the heritage of Anglo-Russian ri-

valry for mastery in Asia, handed down from Tsarist
Russia to Red Russia, gave it sharper edge; but both
as social conflict and power conflict Russian intervention in the Far East was in the logic of its historical
period. Then came the failure of the Western empires
to make any concession to China which might have
warded off the climax; but concessions to subject people are not in the spirit of imperialism while empires
are still strong, and furthermore they entailed the risk
of both political and economic losses which at the end
of a destructive war would be less easily borne. Then
came the failure of the Western empires to do the
obverse of conciliating by concession, namely punish-
ing China for mutiny; but, again, the World War had
left the Western empires too depleted of military
strength and spirit for distant punitive expeditions.
Then, partly by reason of the failure to impose any
check, came China's full challenge for independence,
a challenge that carried a threat to Japan's imperial
pretensions; but this, too, is in the nature of successful
nationalism and it was in application, perhaps, of the
lesson of political experience, which is to wrest advantages when the opponent is weak. Japan being an empire in the ascendant, it could brook no threat to its
pretensions, more particularly at a time when the preliminaries to Europe's new embroilment again seemed
to confer on Japan a free hand for aggrandizement.
And this, too, was part of recent history. Thus step by
step, moving apparently with fatality but actually only
with the spirit of the age, the Far East was carried forward to war, catastrophe and the formation of new
configurations.

CHAPTER III

AT STAKE IN THE CONFLICT

The configurations will be such as to give the whole world a new contour; so much can be said already, even if the final form cannot yet be discerned. The Far East will never again be the same as it was before 1937, and therefore neither will the rest of the world be the same as it was before 1937. The wars in Europe and Asia complement each other in wreaking transformation as well as destruction of the past, but even if there had been no European war the Far Eastern war alone would have left a deep and permanent impress on the Western world. An historical epoch has closed. The day of Western empire in the Far East, if not in the whole East, is done. The hope of the West that the Far East would remain a field for exclusively or even predominantly Western economic exploitation must be renounced. What internal economic and social readjustments the latter will entail for the West remains to be seen; they may be profound and shaking.

In this respect it is immaterial whether Japan or China wins the war, that is, whether China is compelled to submit to a Japanese dominated regime or Japan is compelled to withdraw from China. In either case the sway of Western Powers in the Far East is over and their relationship with Far Eastern lands will be that of countries having political and economic intercourse on terms of equality. What Japan's object is in the event of victory has already been made clear in act and word. It is, in short, the exclusion of the West from the Far East. Prince Konoye's manifesto as Premier on December 22, 1938, enunciating the New Order in East Asia was not so much a declaration of intent as a formal registration of a program already in course of fulfillment. The New Order was to be established for the purpose "of realizing the relationship of neighborly amity, common defense against communism and economic cooperation." To the end of defense against communism Japan would demand, among other things, "that Japanese troops be stationed at specified points [in China]." With regard to economic relations, "China should extend to Japan facilities for the development of China's natural resources, especially in the regions of North China and Inner Mongolia." On two occasions earlier in the same year, when talking under less formal auspices, Prince Konoye had permitted himself to be more explicit and more communicative. On January 22 he said: "In the field of industry the basic principle of the government will be laid in the increase of our nation's productive power under the one comprehensive scheme covering Japan, Manchukuo and China, and efforts are to be exerted toward supplying the articles needed for national defense, promoting all the important industries and expanding our export trade." And on November 3 he was even more revealing. He declared that what Japan desired was a new order. "This new order has for its foundation a tripartite relationship of mutual coordination between Japan, Manchukuo and China in political, economic, cultural and other fields."

Before Prince Konoye spoke Japan's aims could be

deduced from its acts. Had he never spoken, they would be unmistakable in Japan's course since then. The establishment of the Wang Ching-wei government, a palpably Japanese-directed and Japanese-controlled organ; the closing of China's internal waterways to foreign shipping; the manipulation of the Chinese tariff to disqualify imports from the West; the imposition of Japanese exchange control in occupied areas; most of all, the setting up of official and semi-official monopolies over China's more important natural resources and basic economic activities—all these are conclusive. A few such monopolies now have the role of giant holding companies over substantially the whole of China's economy. Politically, then, if Japan is successful, China will be a Japanese domain, whether as colony, protectorate or puppet in the manner of Manchukuo. Economically, too, China will be a Japanese domain. Western trading nations will be denied direct access to the Chinese market and reserves of raw materials. For all practical purposes they will be denied indirect access as well. For the tripartite bloc of which Prince Konoye spoke will be a quasi-autarchic bloc, self-sufficient and self-contained, operating as a managed economy with all the instrumentalities devised by totalitarian systems. The industrial development of China will be "controlled"; that is, organized, paced and directed in accordance with a central scheme laid down by Japan for objects deemed desirable by Japan. It may be taken for granted that the primary object will be the reinforcement of Japan's military strength. To that end China's interests will be subordinated and Western interests in the Far East will have to be sacrificed. The Far East will be a closed world rigidly ruled by a Japanese dictatorship composed of a military caste and its industrial satellites. This is not a matter of forecast or speculation. It is a projection of what already has been set in train. Japanese success signifies the end of the West in the Far East.

The future of Western territorial possessions in Far Eastern waters neighboring China is conditional on the outcome of the European war as well as the Far Eastern war. But it can be said that if Japan is successful in China, only physical restraint by whichever side is victorious in Europe will prevent Japan from extending its sway over the colonies and protectorates now parts of Western empires. If Japan has freedom of action, if, that is, the victors in Europe do not lay an injunction supported by the threat of force, it will appropriate all Western territorial holdings in the Eastern Pacific waters and incorporate them in its continental empire. That Japan will practise moderation in the full flush of success, more particularly when circumstances of international relations create opportunities that may never recur, is hardly to be expected. It would be contrary to the conventions and to the psychology of the Japanese military caste, which is not given to moderation. It would indeed be out of line with Japanese thought. The Japanese have in the past talked of the "southward drive" alternately with expansion on the Asiatic continent. It was a moot point in Japanese controversy on national strategy which should come first, but the argument was on priority, not on mutually exclusive alternatives. The army and the continental school won, and China was invaded first, but the navy and the advocates of expansion southward will come into their own if Germany wins in Europe and is unable or unwilling to veto Japan's absorption of the eastern extremity of the British, French and Dutch empires—unwilling either because the cost is too great or because a bargain has been struck with Japan. In either case Japan will wield the power of one of the great empires of all time and there will be a transposition of political, economic and military power so great as to produce a tremendous shift in the focal point of world affairs. And incidentally, the West will be excluded from more than China. Either this, then, must result from Japan's victory in China or there must be a terrific struggle in the Eastern hemisphere to prevent its consummation.

The West will be forced out of the Far East if Japan wins; it will be forced out, too, if China wins. But in the latter case it will be forced out under circumstances and with a purpose so different as to make the incidence of separation far less onerous. Of the fact itself there can be little doubt. It must be remembered that the train of events leading to the climax in the Far East was set in motion by the advent of Chinese nationalism and the resolve to emancipate the country from infringements on its sovereignty. Chinese nationalism will be strengthened by the war rather than the reverse. China will emerge from the war, if successful, tried by fire and hardened. It will have become conscious of its powers. If it has succeeded in repelling the gravest threat to its independence, made by the strongest of its enemies, it will not be likely then to submit to infringements by countries further away and less strong. It is not likely, in other words, to relapse passively into a state of semi-subjection such as obtained before 1937. To the contrary, escape from conquest by Japan will give it a lift of the spirit which will be more likely to carry it to renewed intransigence. And the opportunity will be favorable. In the first place, what was known as the prestige of the white race is irrecoverably lost. It was forfeited in the complaisant or helpless submission of the white countries to the indignities inflicted on their nationals, the damage done to their properties and the restraints laid on their trade by the Japanese after 1937. For purposes of dramatic simplification it might be said that the prestige of the white race ended in July, 1939, with the stripping of British subjects by grinning Japanese soldiers in Tientsin. The awe that white men once commanded was forever dissipated by those unrequited humiliations. In the second place, the Chinese will perceive with even greater clarity than after 1918 that the Western countries are in no condition after the second European war to undertake distant punitive expeditions. China to the contrary will be left with national energies and resources impaired no doubt but also with a huge army in being, an army steeled and proved by years of fighting. In short, there will be an end to the system of foreign concessions and settlements on Chinese soil, foreign garrisons in Chinese cities, foreign warships in Chinese inland waters, extraterritoriality and foreign supervision of Chinese administrative organs. China will no longer submit to having its territory interspersed by little foreign enclaves that are not only physical contradictions of its sovereignty but also jumping-off places for potential enemies. The system of unequal treaties will pass, by abrogation or desuetude. China will no longer be an outpost of Western empires. It will be independent in fact as well as diplomatic convention.

But to lose territorial possessions, political rights and perquisites is a relatively inconsequential loss unless those possessions, rights and perquisites go to the aggrandizement of other Powers. It represents only a negative retrogression, a kind of devolution of imperial power, which in itself is not fatal or even vital. Indeed, the loss might have been discounted in advance. Despite the romantic and brummagem illusions of the end of the nineteenth century, the callow, brash and pharisaical certitude of the white man's anointment to rule the whole world, the ascendancy of the West was a deviation from the norm rather than the norm. It was episodic, almost factitious—the transitory disparity in military strength and social effectiveness following from earlier industrialization by the West. Once the disparity was redressed, as in the nature of social evolution it had to be, and once the concept of nationalism was disseminated, as in the nature of mechanized communications it had to be, the ascendancy of the West would have to be relaxed. The means of maintaining it would be progressively countered and nullified. The latter was already in train before the war broke out in the Far East. Japan had industrialized to a degree of proficiency which enabled it to compete in the markets of the world, to compete with alarming success in fact. It has long had a military establishment of the same order of effectiveness as the principal world Powers. China had begun to industrialize and to equip itself with modern armament. The challenge to Western imperialism was gathering anyway, a challenge irresistible because it had behind it the logic of history and the instruments of power of its epoch. The Far Eastern war has only brought about a foreshortening of a process which would have worked in any event. In the form in which it works if China becomes master in its own house—and perhaps shows the way to other Oriental dependencies of Western empires—it has consequences that are serious but not disastrous, and that would have had to be reckoned with in any case with the passing of time. But in kind and result this is wholly different from direct eviction by Japan as a matter of force.

The essential points of difference are two. First, exclusion of the Western Powers from the Far East by a Chinese victory will be a loss relative only to their past position and aspirations; none of them will be disadvantaged relative to each other. All will remain on an equal footing in the Far East. There will be no problems raised by newly created empires, no threats to security, no necessity for bases or outposts, no cumulative tensions. There will be no necessity to prepare to fight to preserve Eastern possessions or to extend imperial frontiers as a defensive measure. In fact, since the disputed areas of the earth will be by so much circumscribed, benefits will accrue in the form of economies on armament, to say nothing of the benefit of being at least to some extent absolved from the horrors of war. In this respect a Chinese victory and a

Japanese victory would have diametrically opposite results.

The second point of difference is more direct in its bearing and more important. In the event of a Chinese victory the Western Powers will be deprived of political special privileges but not of economic opportunity. There will be no Asiatic "bloc," no autarchy, no "rationalization" of the economy for purposes of greater military power, no sealing up the area against foreign economic intrusion. There will be no inducement to adopt such measures. The pressure will be in the opposite direction. To be sure, China will never again be the economic happy hunting ground for foreigners that it once was. The Chinese tariff will never again be framed with a view primarily to the interests of foreign traders. Foreign banks established in Chinese ports will no longer exercise a quasi-monopoly of credit. Foreign persons and property will no longer enjoy an idyllic immunity from taxation. Nor will they have the most advantageous sites, regulations that inure to their interests and China's detriment and a multiplicity of priorities as once they did. They will occupy the same positions they do wherever they live and do business as aliens. Nor will they enjoy the monopoly in purveying manufactured goods they once had and counted on having forever. All that is over; but it would have passed in any case, with the industrialization first of Japan and then of China. It could have been preserved only by force or threat of force. But with China recovering independence, determined to cast off trammels and conscious of the indispensability of modernization, it will go by fiat. This is, however, far from exclusion from economic opportunity.

It is precisely in the industrialization of China that there lies the most promising opportunity for profitable enterprise by foreign countries, an opportunity that no imperialistic domination could yield, an opportunity such as perhaps has never existed hitherto except when the American continent was being developed. Here indeed may lie the hope of escape, at least for a period, from the economic impasse in which Western industrialized countries have been caught for more than a decade. For China to be developed industrially it will need credit; it will need capital goods. There will be thousands of miles of railways to be built, mines to be opened, harbors to be dug and equipped, public utilities to be established, factories of all kinds to be furnished with machinery. The banks and workshops of the world can be kept profitably occupied for decades if China is unimpeded in industrializing.

It is true that much lavish rhetoric has been aired in the past about the El Dorado in China and that the elaborate expectations thus implied have not materialized. But from this it does not follow that there are not prodigious possibilities of trade expansion in China; it follows only that rhetoric is baseless in economic calculations. The market that China has constituted up to the present and that has failed to come up to illusory expectations, that is, a market for consumers' goods only, has of course limitations—in China as elsewhere. The roseate prophecies of an ever increasing sale of goods to China because its population was enormous naturally could come to nothing so long as China was a country of subsistence farming and handicraft production. Its purchasing power was limited by the volume and value of its raw materials. The commercial potentialities of any country, whether large or small, come into play only when it begins to industrialize. For only then do its demands extend beyond a narrow range of cheap commodities and only then can it pay proportionately. When it is so cogently argued, as has become the fashion in recent Far Eastern polemics, that the Chinese market has proved a false hope, all that is said is that China's industrialization has been delayed. The same would be true of any country in which industrialism was retarded. But in a country as large as China, with as stubbornly rooted a culture as China's and suffering from as many impediments and restraints as have been laid on China in the years of semi-subjection, a fundamental change in the nature of society, in the structure and spirit of the civilization, had to come slowly. Under the circumstances the delay was not abnormally protracted. It is less than fifty years since the West moved into China in force and the appeal of the Chinese market became a factor in political calculations, and fifty years is a short time as time is measured in social change. It must be remembered that although Japan is generally credited with miracles in its social transformation, it was entering into the stage of effective industrialism only at the time of the first World War, also nearly fifty years after it had begun. If judgment on Japan's role in world trade had been taken on the basis of 1900, thirty years after it had begun to

modernize, it could also have been said that Japan had
no trade possibilities; but now Japan is America's
third best customer. It is considerably less than thirty
years since China really began to industrialize; actually
it is scarcely more than ten, and in the few years before 1937 China had made notable strides. But it has
begun, and, if not obstructed by obstacles over which
it has no control, which means in effect conquest by
Japan or domination by Soviet Russia, it will press
on with increasing vigor. Only thereafter will it be
determined how much China offers the rest of the
world by way of market. But on all the logic of modern
society and by all the precedents of every other land
which has come into the system of mechanized production, the provision of capital goods for the development of half a continent inhabited by more than 400,-
000,000 persons should offer opportunity to the already
industrialized nations on a scale which has seldom been
surpassed.

It is true also that the opportunity will be of limited
duration. In the passing of time and in direct proportion to China's efficiency in modernization, China will
follow the course of other economically backward nations which have industrialized. Its plant fully
equipped, both as to production and distribution, it
will cease depending on the outer world, first for consumers' goods, then for capital goods, then for credit
as its own surplus capital accumulates. First it will
supply its own needs, and then, having acquired
enough proficiency to produce a surplus, it will enter
into competition for other markets with the nations
which before were its suppliers. This has been the

course of Japan; it has been the course of the United States; it will be the course of China or of any other country which newly industrializes.

The relationship between more advanced countries and an economically backward country started on development can always be described by the same curve. First there is a rise in the export of consumers' goods —textiles, trinkets, simpler articles of commercial and domestic use, small tools and implements, gadgets. The rise tends to become steeper as the backward people acquire the new demands, a process which works cumulatively. Then the curve tends to flatten as the native people are tempted by the profits they see being made from the purveyance of such goods and learn to produce them themselves—textiles always in the first instance and then other commodities that can be made with less complicated tools in small shops which are essentially household industry with small power-driven implements. Then as the native people acquire greater technical proficiency and more individuals are technically trained, and there is a growing conviction among the educated classes that the nation must industrialize, the curve rises sharply again, for then new communications systems must be laid, power plants set up, roads and highways extended, factories erected and machinery installed. This is the stage at which the more advanced countries reap their harvest, the stage in which their economy is expanding. Then the curve flattens again, as the newly developing country has enough of an industrial establishment to begin making its own capital goods and then to reach out for markets outside its own boundaries, first in textiles and cheap commodities, after the fashion of the countries from which it formerly bought. Then the curve may even decline, as the advanced countries are displaced first in its own market and then in other markets to which it is nearer and in which it has the advantage of lower costs of transportation. The decline may not be continuous, for as a nation enters fully into the industrial system it may compete at some points but its own needs increase, its trade becomes more complex and the total value of the trade with older countries may not diminish. In fact, as multilateral trade is extended by its own development, it may even buy more than it ever did. The economic relations between England and Germany and England and the United States so appear to indicate. Whether that is true only because there were ever newer regions to reach out into as England was displaced by Germany in the German markets and then in other markets cannot be conclusively determined; there may be rigid limits to the scope of expansion for industrial societies. At any rate there is clearly a period in which there is a levelling off in exports to newly developed countries and adjustment must be made for competition with them. It will be so in China too. But clearly the process is a long one, and between the time when China starts industrializing, which is now, and the time when it need no longer buy capital goods from the other countries and can compete with them, decades must elapse, decades in which the industrialized countries can prosper from their trade with China. Beyond that period it is impossible to calculate, and unnecessary to calculate. Within that period the economic system based on machine production will have ample time to evolve to a basis of stability and will be under the necessity of doing so.

It is true, further, that the benefits from the development of China must accrue in larger part to Japan, since Japan has the advantages of nearness to the Chinese market and a greater similarity of language, customs and habits. This is inescapable, fixed in the nature of geography and following from the fact that in the nature of contemporary civilization nothing could have prevented Japan from industrializing. But even if this be true, given the free play of economic forces there will still be a large access of trade for Western countries even if Japan has the larger share. For Japan cannot yet provide all China's needs; at that stage its own industrial establishment has not yet arrived, nor has it all the raw materials that would be requisite. Even if Japan has the larger share directly, indirectly Western countries will still be selling more to China, since Japan will have to continue to buy raw materials, semi-manufactured products and machinery with which to make the goods that it will sell to China. There will still be much for Western countries. If, that is—*if* economic forces continue to have free play. This condition is at the heart of the whole economic question raised by the Far Eastern conflict, perhaps at the heart of the political question as well. It must be discussed at this point, for it will have much to do with determining decisions as to policy by Western countries and has already exercised some influence in forming opinion. While it has not been overtly discussed in public controversy on the Far East since 1937, it has weighed in the minds of those concerned with the Far East, whether as governments or business groups. It has served as the stuff of mental reservations about the effect of Japan's attempt to conquer China, and for certain groups has provided an argument on which to reconcile themselves to the absorption of China into Japan's political and economic system.

This argument needs to be examined. It runs roughly as follows. However objectionable Japanese conquest may be morally and whatever risks it may hold politically, from the point of view of material interests it makes little difference to the West whether Japan conquers or not. So far as there is any difference, a Japanese victory may actually be of material advantage to the West, since Japanese occupation and control will mean a faster development of China's natural resources. True, the West will participate in the ensuing profits at one remove. But the profits to be shared will be greater than those conceivable without the help of Japanese "law and order." True, also, American, British and other Western enterprises will be evicted from China as they have been from Manchukuo, and foreign interests will henceforth have to use Japanese concerns as intermediaries. Yet through Japan the West will be able to sell more to China than it does now and it will be able to invest more capital in China than it does now.

Japan is efficient, technologically advanced and experienced in industrial and financial organization; China is inexperienced and inefficient. Japan can ensure stable government in China; the Chinese cannot. The industrialization of China thus will be accelerated under Japanese control, whereas with continued Chinese independence it will lag, as it has for decades. The great Chinese market, thus far a myth, will become a reality. Open Door or no Open Door, without industrialization the Chinese market will remain meager, to be picked at on the edges for scant findings. With industrialization, which is possible under Japanese tutelage, which in turn is possible only under Japanese political control, the purchasing power of China's huge population can be expanded and the world will find the commercial outlet it so sorely needs. Western firms and individuals now established in China will suffer, of course. But to European and American industry as a whole, and to European and American factory workers, it matters little whether European and American products are sold to China directly through European and American firms or indirectly through Japanese firms. The banker, industrialist and worker at home benefit equally either way, so long as the products are sold. And if Japan can stabilize China, organize it and develop it, they will benefit immeasurably more, because immeasurably more products will be sold.

The argument has a plausible ring; it has the ring of sound economic theory; but it is dubious, if not altogether fallacious. It rests on two assumptions, both of which are at least challengeable and on all contemporary evidence contrary to fact. They are, first, that the acceleration of China's industrialization under Japanese control and the resulting increase in China's demand for goods from abroad will be great enough to compensate other countries for the loss of direct access to the Chinese market, and, second, that Japan will not prevent artificially the equitable diffusion of the benefits arising from China's industrial development.

With respect to the first: when one talks of acceleration one talks in terms of a comparison of the rate of development of China if Japan wins and what will happen in any event. For it is clear that China will make some industrial progress without regard to its political state. As has been said, China had already begun to industrialize and was advancing rapidly before 1937. That China lacks Japan's technical proficiency and would require years to attain it is undeniable. There are tremendous social and political obstacles to overcome, old institutions to modify or uproot, new ones to create. Further, China is handicapped by lack of free capital, though this is not irremediable. Given a continuation of progress toward political unification and stabilization such as marked the few years before 1937, China would have had little difficulty in raising loans abroad. And if it can be presumed that the undoubted coalescence of the war years will endure after a victory which leaves the country independent then, too, China will have little difficulty in raising loans abroad. Indeed, in this respect Japan may henceforth be more handicapped than China unless Europe and America come to its assistance. It is at least arguable that foreign lenders would be less reluctant to lend to a victorious and unified China than to a Japan victorious over China but left in a precarious domestic position as a result of a costly and prolonged war, which by normal calculations, has already reduced

Japan to insolvency. A victorious China might very well be a better risk than a victorious Japan. Not being an industrialized country with a highly articulated economy, China is less sensitive in all its parts to what happens in any one of them, and therefore will not be left prostrated by the war. Its recuperative faculties will be less impaired. If, then, China wins, it will proceed from the point at which it was interrupted by the outbreak of the war, probably with added impetus gained from the clearing away of social obstacles in the war, from the heightened morale generated by the war, from the confidence and experience gained in sustaining itself though shut off from the world by the blockade, as exemplified in Western China. In many ways China has been finding itself economically since 1937. With all the factors that operate against China conceded, there are now other factors to counter-balance them, if not yet to cancel them out. Given an opportunity, China will move forward again in modernization, moving with an ever increasing momentum. The tide of social evolution is set in that direction.

The argument might even be made that this tide will be arrested if Japan should defeat China and then take over both the economy and the government of the country. Japan will begin with its own resources depleted. Surplus capital, already decreased by the expenditures in Manchukuo and the armament program indispensable to safeguarding the subsequent continental position, will be exhausted. Japan, too, will need years for recuperation. Moreover, Japan will then have to undertake the reconstruction of China in the midst of an embittered and hostile population, at least a part of which can be expected to continue some form of resistance for years. Japan's resources and energies, or what is left of them after the war, will have to be divided between the attempt to develop China and the unavoidable task of pacifying and policing the country. It can be confidently predicted that the larger share of both will go toward pacification and policing. This will be true whether Japan is spending its own money or money borrowed from abroad. Any credits advanced to Japan will be used for completing the subjugation of China as well as for developing a market in China for foreign goods.

Japan must complete the conquest of China, guard against recurrent uprisings and at the same time set about the construction of an administrative mechanism extending over half a continent and governing more than 400,000,000 people. It must do these, too, before it can proceed with building railways, opening mines, erecting factories and carrying out other projects requiring raw materials and machinery from abroad. In sum, against all the factors making for accelerated development of China under Japanese auspices and a consequent increase in China's demand for foreign goods can be set just as many factors that make for retardation of China's development under Japan. That China's economic progress was checked by the war is certain. There are good grounds for believing that it will be checked even more drastically if Japan wins.

It is at least doubtful, too, whether the higher rate of development under Japan would be enough to compensate for the losses sustained by the West by exclusion from direct access to China. That there would be such exclusion is unnecessary to demonstrate. Korea and Manchukuo stand to witness. Japanese practices in the last generation are conclusive evidence. No overt acts would be necessary, not even such as have characterized the period following 1937. No official edicts of eviction or restaint would be required. As already has been said, there would be devices such as tariff schedules and customs rulings, import and export regulations, currency controls and credit manipulations, all operating to debar Occidentals. Chinese would be intimidated from continuing to deal with Occidentals by threats to cut off their credit, supplies of goods, transportation facilities, etc. In addition there would be all the oblique devices at which the Japanese are adept—freight cars with foreign shipments mysteriously delayed or lost, foreign cargoes mysteriously damaged in unloading at wharves or fined for mysterious breaches of customs regulations, foreign factories subjected to unceasing inspections and found in violation of recondite regulations previously unheard of. The cumulative effect would be to leave foreign enterprises no reason for remaining in China. They would not have to be physically expelled. The Japanese would have to speed up China's development at a rate hardly to be looked for if the account is to be balanced.

All this, however, is secondary. What matters more is the validity of the second assumption, with respect to the free play of economic forces without the interposition of extraneous impediments by Japan. It cannot be disputed that if normal economic processes were allowed to function in accordance with traditional economic law, the increment from China to all industrial countries would be the same no matter whether China was sovereign or Japan. The same quantity of steel rails, motors, locomotives, machine tools, oil and cotton would then be required for China whether the government of China was Chinese or Japanese. Goods would, in the latter case, merely be sold to China through Japan. The increase of prosperity accruing to Japan from its profits in China would be reflected in Japan's increased purchases from Western countries. The addition to Japan's wealth might be employed in investment in other Far Eastern regions, increasing the purchasing power of these regions and Japan's purchasing power through them. The volume of goods interchanged and, therefore, produced would be larger or at least as large. The question of who happened to act as intermediate agents in the transactions would be of minor importance.

Such a result depends, however, on the functioning of normal economic processes. But what reason is there to believe that they will be permitted to function if Japan wins? All the tendencies in Japan's own economic organization in recent years and the declarations of ruling Japanese groups are in the opposite direction, indeed, almost constrain Japan in the opposite direction. These give little reason to believe that Japan will undertake the task of developing China's natural resources with the main purpose of unlocking those resources to the world as soon as it can, giving the inhabitants a higher standard of living and thus opening the market as widely as possible. There is no evidence that Japan has any plans for

China that can be so described. To the contrary, enough has already been quoted earlier in this chapter to show what Japan's officially declared purposes are —a tripartite bloc embracing China, administered as a centrally controlled economy with all the instrumentalities of a "planned" economy, as military totalitarianism construes planning. And the great monopolistic holding companies such as the North China Development Company and the Central China Development Company, which are official or semi-official companies—meaning, of course, enterprises controlled by the military—are more indicative than governmental pronouncements.

What is it that Japan wants to get from China and will get if it has the power? Raw materials mainly: iron, coal, salt and above all cotton, in order to emancipate itself from dependence on American cotton supply. In the scheme of the integrated tripartite bloc China's role is that of reservoir of raw materials. Its population would remain predominantly a peasant population. Only such light industries would be established as can produce consumers' goods for local use more cheaply than they can be produced in Japan. No industries would be established that compete with Japan's. In short, Japan would be the manufactory, China the source of supply of raw materials. What, then, is offered to Western interests? What machinery would they sell—how many automobiles, tractors, harvesters, turbines, typewriters, lathes, punch presses? Without a balanced industrialization and the earning power that goes with industrialization, what would the Chinese use to pay for imported articles? Peasants live at subsistence level. Japan would organize the production of the area to yield such raw materials as it needs and as much as it needs, striking some equation between what it needs and what the region must produce to exchange for the cheap manufactures that Japan expects to sell there. All the instrumentalities of exchange control, control of investments, quotas, bounties and subsidies would be employed to bring about such a balance—a balance as between China and Japan. And the ultimate criterion would be the effect on Japan's military strength.

Western countries will have no place in China under Japanese dominion. China—whether as colony, protectorate or "independent" ally of Japan after the fashion of Manchukuo—will not be altogether closed to Western enterprise. A little trade may penetrate through the interstices left by Japan's own deficiencies in raw materials. A certain amount of steel will be sold for, say, the railways that Japan decides to build either to export certain natural resources or to satisfy its strategic necessities. Japan may permit the sale of capital goods which it is not yet able to produce itself and which it thinks it must have right away. Other countries may be called on to supply what the Japanese quasi-totalitarian regime requires to attain its ends. But no more; and much more than this Western countries could expect in the normal course if China were to remain independent, even though its independent development might not be so spectacular as it might be in the first years under Japanese domination. On balance, then, Western countries have nothing to gain from Japan's success in China and much to lose. And for them to adopt policies or advance credits to Japan in the belief that Japan will act as their pioneer traveling salesman in Eastern Asia would be to underwrite their own undoing.

The fundamental question that must be attached to this analysis, whether Japan's program is feasible in itself and without regard to action taken by other countries, is not germane in this connection but must be taken cognizance of. It may be the central point on which the fate of Japan's empire and the political cast of the Far East turn. No such program has been feasible in any other part of the world. It could not work under a free economic system such as obtained throughout the period of modern imperialism, and except by the devices of totalitarianism it could not work now. Whether it can do so even with the aid of those devices must remain conjectural until we know from the test of time whether they are ephemeral, the symptoms of a transitory fevered period which will pass when the social organism regains its health, or they are to remain as the governing principle and method of operation in the social organization of the future. But even in the latter case Japan may still find itself in the same position vis-à-vis China as the older industrialized countries now occupy vis-à-vis the East, Japan included.

When Japanese productivity rises and the pressure to dispose of surplus products becomes irresistible, it will be found desirable to dispose of them in China. The allocation of functions between China and Japan may not prove practicable. If China is kept as a storehouse of raw materials, its ability to absorb much of Japan's manufactured production is limited. It would be limited even if China had an unprecedented plenitude of raw materials, as it has not. If China's purchasing power is restricted to its supply of raw materials, then there is a limit to Japan's exports of manufactured products, unless Japan can export the surplus to still other countries. In doing so Japan will have the advantage of being able to dictate the price it pays for Chinese raw materials and having a cheap labor supply, but it will have the disadvantage of being compelled to surmount tariff and other barriers levelled against it in proportion to its efforts to "dump" in other markets.

It will then be desirable and perhaps necessary to dispose of surplus products in China. To that end China's purchasing power will have to be raised— raised in the only way that it can be raised, namely, by fostering machine industry in China. The temptation to sell producers' goods in China will not be resisted, just as England could not resist the temptation to sell power looms and spindles to Japan. Thus Japan in China will be setting up competition with Japan proper—and the cycle of imperialistic expansion everywhere will have set in. Japan can break through this cycle in one way only. It might avert the complications and obstacles of international payments by incorporating the whole of Chinese territory into its own realm, China constituting just so many provinces of Japan. But in view of China's greater area, population and resources, the political and economic center of gravity of the expanded realm would shift to the continent and Japan proper would in time become a province of the new realm, even if the name of the empire remained Japan. This might be economically and politically practicable and sound; psychologically it is impossible. That the Japanese would voluntarily allow such a process to work to its logical conclusion is not credible. They will doubtless prefer the traditional course, even if it sets in the cycle which at least economically has worked toward a devolution of the great empires of the nineteenth century and made imperialism self-defeating inwardly, however successful in the externalities of power. From this Japan can save itself only by effective totalitarianism. And even effective totalitarianism may not be sufficient. But whether Japan's program is ultimately practicable or not, Japan will attempt to execute it, if it has the opportunity, if, that is, it conquers China. And in the interval before impracticability is demonstrated, the West will have been denied opportunity in China, and will have to choose between loss by default or preservation of interest by battle.

CHAPTER IV

CONDITIONS TO LASTING PEACE

This study began by asking what is the basis of a lasting peace in the Far East. If the foregoing analysis is sound the answer follows by compelling logic. It is clear at least on what basis there can *not* be peace in the Far East. There can be no peace, stability or even order in the Far East or, for that matter, anywhere in the world if Japan can establish control over China. The first and indispensable condition to a lasting settlement is, then, the defeat of Japan in the present war. By defeat is meant the withdrawal of all Japanese troops from China—Manchuria included—and the acceptance of a relationship with China confined to ordinary diplomatic intercourse and trade as between any two independent countries. Whether this is brought about by China's ability to repel the invaders or by Japan's economic exhaustion or by the intervention of one or more Powers, sooner or later, in one way or another, it must be brought about. If not, there must be war, perhaps recurrent war: war among the surviving empires for redivision of the territorial spoils in the Far East, the motives being security and power; war among the great trading nations for the largest share of the profits from the exploitation of Eastern lands, the motive being economic necessity or advantage. The fixed point from which any effort to deal with the Far East must proceed is the frustration of Japan's design for continental empire, with withdrawal from China as the criterion.

To restrain Japan is a condition precedent; but it is negative only. A basis for peace must be laid in something more positive. There is prerequisite, too, the converse of Japanese defeat, namely, Chinese victory in the present war. By victory is meant clearing Chinese territory of Japanese troops and then, what is of equal importance, restoring to China substantive as well as juridical sovereignty. This calls for measures that run against Western countries no less than against Japan. It means the voluntary abandonment of the territorial, political and economic positions maintained by Western countries in China up to the present. Concretely, such concessions and settlements as remain must be retroceded; fighting ships in Chinese waters and garrisons on Chinese soil must be withdrawn; extraterritoriality must be waived. European and American nationals must be content with a relationship of equality, residing in China subject to Chinese laws and trading with China as with any other independent country. All this may proceed in graduated stages to cushion the shock of readjustment, but it must be set in motion at once, whenever Japan begins to withdraw. As the withdrawal of Japanese troops is designed to restore the status quo ante 1931 as a condition of peace, so the abandonment of the Western position in China is designed to restore the status quo 1842. For to have peace in the Far East it is necessary to go back more than ten years. It is necessary to go back to the beginning of Occidental-Chinese relations in their modern phase. A century must be undone, if the consequences of that century as now tragically visible are not to run on.

Nothing less than this can extricate the Far East from the imperialistic war system, for unless China ceases to be a prize of conquest no settlement of this or any similar war in the future can serve as more than interlude. Conclusive conquest of China could not foreclose the conflict. Aside from the question whether China would remain permanently submissive, the other challengers would not be eliminated. Japan is not and cannot for a long period become strong enough to put itself beyond challenge. In this respect it is immaterial how the European war ends. If the British and French empires survive, they will not permit their interests in China to go by default, once they have recovered from the war. Still more, they will not permit their Eastern possessions neighboring China to be permanently overshadowed and subject to threat. Sooner or later they will seek to rehabilitate themselves in the East; they will have to, if they are to remain world empires. At the same time the United States will have become heavily armed and apprehensive, both to a greater degree than ever before in its history. Soviet Russia will be more vigilant in the East than before. With permutations determined by balance of power politics, combinations will be formed with and against Japan in Far Eastern expansion.

If on the other hand Germany and Italy win and Great Britain and France are eliminated, there may be an allocation of spoils at the beginning among ostensibly amicable victors, with perhaps China and the larger share of other Eastern colonies awarded to

Japan. But it will be a transitory bargain rather than a settlement, an uneasy truce rather than peace. With Germany, Italy and Japan all empires on the make, each seeking to stake out as much as it can for itself before the more valuable areas are appropriated and incorporated into strong competing systems, no one of them is likely contentedly to foreswear the most tempting prizes to partners by the momentary exigencies of power politics. Least of all would Germany, when its hour of destiny had struck, be inclined to renounce the pearl of the East—to Japan above all. To do so would not be in the psychology of successful imperialism, in the psychology of German arms when successful or in consonance with the racial myth that nourishes the spirit of the Third Reich.

As for Soviet Russia, if it should enter into any agreement on partition or allotment of spheres or accept any such agreement among the three other parties it will do so with mental reservations. For to do otherwise would hardly comport with the philosophy of the world revolution, if Soviet Russia is still a revolutionary state, and still less with historic Russian imperial ambitions, if Soviet Russia is now just another empire, an expanding state moving by the weight of its military power. In either case permanent acceptance of Japanese dominion over Eastern Asia, with or without German and Italian participation, is irreconcilable with Russian ideas or Russian destiny. Principles of totalitarian social organization are all that Germany, Italy, Japan and Russia have in common. Mutual trust they have not. They have no common aspirations. To the contrary, their ambitions are inherently in conflict. Even with Russia left out of account as falling in a distinctive political category and Italy left out of account as negligible except for a momentary and factitious importance deriving from its attachment as pendant to a rising German empire, the ambitions and intentions of Japan and Germany are mutually so antagonistic as to make a genuine and lasting division of possessions and perquisites between them impossible. Always, moreover, the United States must be taken into account—in still another category, not yet irrevocably committed to being immured between its two ocean walls and perhaps never to find it possible so to commit itself, if only for reasons formed by the imperious demands of its economy. Perhaps as much as any other nation the United States must be taken into account in the Pacific. And only when it is resigned to isolation on its own continent will the United States accede to a settlement in the Far East which allocates China to Japan exclusively or to Japan and its allies.

Even with the elimination of Great Britain and France, then, there can be no peace in the Far East with China still in subjection or semi-subjection, a prize of conquest. There can only be transitory arrangements in disposal, determined by shifting combinations of Powers, the most likely in the immediate future being between Germany and Japan, if Germany should become master of Europe. But aside from the internal incompatibilities in such a combination, it would generate counter-combinations after the fashion of power politics, until there was decision by battle.

No matter what historical transformations are in

the making in imperial power and social organization through the wars in Europe and Asia, the fundamental principle still holds: China can no longer be a stake in power politics if there is to be peace in the Far East. Without regard to the outcome in Europe, peace in the Far East requires in the first instance that Japan be curbed, then that the Western Powers relinquish their outposts in China and then that China be made independent and, furthermore, be strengthened so that it can safeguard the integrity of its soil by its own efforts.

Western withdrawal from China is necessary for two reasons. First, so long as there are foreign encroachments on its soil China will be unremitting in its efforts to rid itself of them unless held down by force. There will be periodic incidents of increasing magnitude until compromise on the merits of individual disputes is no longer possible. At length one Power or another will have to do that which Japan has been attempting to do, and there will be full-scale war. For without force no nation can any longer impinge on China's sovereignty. Sooner or later one issue must be settled. Is China to be wholly independent or wholly a colony, and, if the latter, a colony subject to what empire? On this issue there have already been numerous minor collisions and two major wars since 1900. There will continue to be minor collisions and major wars until it is finally settled, whether now or in the future.

The second reason for the necessity of Western withdrawal from China is that so long as there are Western outposts on the mainland within striking distance of Japan there will be no remission from Japanese efforts to establish hegemony over China. And Japan will be acting in the interests of security as well as out of chauvinism and lust for conquest. Successful aggression, though undertaken originally as a means of defense, may breed a zest for aggression for its own sake, as undoubtedly it has in the case of Japan; but the originating motive may still be one of defense. From the beginning of its expansionist career Japan has been actuated by fear as much as by anything else. When Japanese apologists now say, in defending the New Order in East Asia, that Western influence must be uprooted out of the Far East so that "the peace of East Asia may be stabilized," their premises are sound, even if the logic is warped to arrive at the conclusion that therefore Japan must be conqueror over China. There is the same logical quirk in construing the so-called Monroe Doctrine for East Asia as an enabling act for setting up puppet governments dangling from strings held by the Japanese army. If the Japanese confined themselves to laying injunctions against any further Occidental colonization in China or surrounding regions and stipulating that within a measurable period all Occidental territorial holdings in China be retroceded as being prejudicial to Far Eastern autonomy and stability, their position would be unexceptionable from any broad social point of view. It would be just. It would contribute to the welfare of both the Far East and the West. It would mark an advance in international relations. It would also apply the genuine logic of Japan's position and remove the ground for Japan's fear.

On any objective examination of Far Eastern history it is clear that one of the major factors in that history has been Japan's sense of insecurity, political and military insecurity. Insecurity has been Japan's goad. Japan has never felt sure of its strength or of its status in the world. Psychologically it has never recovered from the stigma of inferiority placed upon it in common with other Eastern, non-white races in the years when Western imperialism and arrogance were at their height. To a great extent its recent aggressions are compensation for its own chagrin and satisfaction wrung from those who inflicted humiliation on it. Politically Japan has never been freed from the spectre raised by the implacable advance of the white empires in the decades before 1900, an advance overwhelming the East as it moved. The vanguard of Western conquest had arrived at China's shores and thus stood on a springboard from which it might leap to Japan at will, when the Japanese in self-preservation fought Russia and won. With victory Japan stemmed the advance, and the World War brought it permanently to a halt—unless the Communist International can be said to have set it going again. But in the memory of that fateful hour of its history Japan's political thinking is formed and its foreign policy cast.

The preventive offensive is the first principle of Japan's political strategy. As long as Western empires retain their advance bases, they may use them as springboards again. One would have to be more credulous than a Japanese militarist to believe that all Western Powers have irrevocably foresworn expansionist aims in the Far East; even before the rise of fascism one could not have been so credulous. At any rate Japan has never believed that the peril is removed and cannot so believe until there is no direct Western political influence in China. But if Japan is not strong enough to give the challenge direct to all of the Western Powers, it can take the oblique approach—forestall them by arrogating China to itself, thus automatically nullifying the utility of the advance bases of the West. . . . And with Japan as with other countries, appetite comes with eating and success begets further boldness. The motives become mixed and the lust for conquest as conquest prevails; but even if it does not, Japan will never become quiescent so long as those bases remain in China, and the appeal of its most egregious militarists will have a certain validity in Japanese popular judgment. The Western nations will come as prejudiced witnesses and their adjurations to Japan to refrain from anti-social conduct in international relations will be suspect and fall on deaf ears. In fact, so long as Western countries have a foothold in China the disestablishment of the military caste from control over the Japanese state and society will be difficult, if not impossible. In a sense, every European concession in China has been and is a stronghold of the Japanese army.

The first requisite is that Japan be curbed. The second is that Western Powers renounce their possessions and special interests in China. The third is that China must become or be made strong enough to safeguard its integrity and to prevent encroachments in the future which would set in motion the same process that brought the Far East to its present state. No larger

purpose would be served by China's escape from subjection to Japan if thereby only one contender were
removed and China remained a passive agent and a
free field for foreign intrusion. Nor would any larger
purpose be served if China were saved from Japan at
the price of being laid under such an obligation to one
or more Powers that in effect it would be in mortgage
again. In international politics only the strong can afford obligations. For this reason, from the point of
view of a durable peace nothing would have been
gained if one or more Powers had intervened in 1937
to stop the Japanese invasion. That would have been
only an estoppal in imperialistic interests. China would
still have been a token; it would simply have been
demonstrated that the token was not permitted to
pass into Japanese hands. (International intervention
under the authority of a system of collective security
would have been a different matter, but there was no
system of collective security.) More particularly, from
the point of view of lasting peace it was better that
neither the United States nor Soviet Russia, the two
countries most directly in question, intervened at
that time. In either case both motive and result could
have been construed merely as decision in a long-
standing rivalry for primacy in the Pacific. And if
Russia had been the means of repelling Japan conflict
would have formed on a new line, a line drawn on
social as well as political issues. China's status vis-à-vis
the world of strong military Powers would have been
unchanged—an object of diplomatic and military ma-
neuvers.

Seen in the long perspective and judged by the cri-

terion of the greatest good in the long run, it was
better that China withstood the full force of the Japanese attack alone, engaged the whole of Japan's strength
and for at least three years prevented the consummation of a Japanese victory. In a calculation taken for
decades rather than these years it was even for China
an economy of human suffering. For now China may
not have to repeat the experience of the years since
1937. Now, no matter what combination of circumstances may lead to action by third Powers, the credit
for repelling Japan is China's. They would intervene
more nearly as allies than as benefactors, later pre-
senting bills for payment. China bore the brunt of
the struggle alone and in so doing acquired confidence
in its own strength and a sense of self-reliance. In the
psychology of modern world politics China matured
between 1937 and 1940. If international exigencies
permitted, third Powers could now throw their weight
into the scale against Japan with less danger that
China and Japan would be repressed alike or Japan
be expelled only for the benefit of some third Power.
But if the danger is to be eliminated altogether, then
even if Japan is compelled either by external force
or internal economic exhaustion to evacuate China,
China must not be left so exhausted that it is helpless.
Or, if it is helpless, then material help must be given
it.

If, however, China is not exhausted, if its governmental mechanism is intact and its army in being, it
can withstand pressure even from its helpful friends.
In this connection the question of Soviet Russia is
specifically in point. Soviet Russia, too, is a neighbor

of China and as a neighbor can be either a source of
help or a menace. Japan, further, has its own feud with
Russia. If Russia decides formally to intervene in the
Far Eastern war, either to further the cause of the
world revolution or to extend the Russian empire to
the Pacific or just to finish off Japan when Japan is
at its weakest, it is essential that Russia be confined
to finishing off Japan. There is no more likelihood
of peace with a Russian-dominated China than with
a Japanese-dominated China. If the British and French
empires survive, then for reasons too obvious to be
elaborated they will not long submit to a Russianized
Asia overshadowing their own Eastern possessions.
They would least likely submit if it were a communized as well as a Russianized Asia. If Europe is a
solid fascist mass there is little more likelihood of acceptance of a Russianized Asia, and still less if it is
a communized Asia. And China itself will be torn by
dissensions, sharper and leading to more bloodshed
than those of the last two decades. The internecine
struggle would be more terrible in that each side
would have external support. There would be a repetition of Spain in 1937 on a vaster scale. This can be
avoided either if Russia is not alone in contributing
to the curbing of Japan or if China is strong enough
to keep external influence at bay, no matter from what
direction. Or, if the threat should come from a victorious Germany and Italy in full career of expansion, the
same would hold true. It would be a lesser threat,
since Germany and Italy are further away than Russia, but nevertheless the most effective preventive
would be China's own strength, toughened by the war

and not yet worn away by attrition. If, however, China is worn down, then support must come from some quarter—diplomatic support, economic support and potential military support. The potentiality of the latter might be enough. And here America enters, though how effective a role America can play must be determined by the result in Europe and the proportions in which America must allocate its strength as between the Atlantic and Pacific.

In sum, the first measures for peace in the Far East are the evacuation of China by Japan, the withdrawal of the Western Powers from their pre-1937 position in China, the avoidance of any obligation of China to any one Power even in return for rescue, and the prevention of China's exhaustion even at the end of a victorious war or the provision of support if it is exhausted. None of these measures may be practicable now. The reshaping of Europe and the repercussions in the Pacific, principally by way of a fascist world alliance, may leave both present and future in the Far East to the arbitrament of force alone. In that case there is no hope of establishing peace in the Far East now. But whether now or later these are the measures by which a foundation for peace can be laid. If there is to be more than foundation, then more constructive measures are required, measures having in view the future interests of Japan and China and taking into consideration the internal structure of both countries. For they will continue at peace only if their societies are viable. It is necessary, then, to turn to an examination of internal problems in both countries.

CHAPTER V

JAPAN'S LEGITIMATE NEEDS

The truism that no nation will remain more passive than its physical weakness dictates unless assured of the means of livelihood has been distorted for purposes of propaganda by the current play on such words as lebensraum, life-lines, population pressure; but in its genuine meaning it is still valid. It applies to Japan no less than to other countries—no less, but also no more, despite the common over-emphasis on Japan's economic needs as an explanation of its political policies. Japan's population problem has become a catchword in all discussion on the Far East, so much so as to falsify the issues. Japan's population problem does not differ in kind from that of any other country. It differs only in the degree of its urgency, and this difference is not enough to give any distinctive content to Far Eastern international relations.

The whole over-emphasis in recent political polemics on the importance of population is dubious and has been unfortunate. For important as considerations arising out of population may be biologically and perhaps sociologically, it may be argued that in international relations they are negligible. It may be argued further that since the passing of the social environment out of which Malthus drew his conclusions population has ceased to be a dynamic of national political movement except in ex post facto apologetics. What is an over-populated country in our time? It is one which cannot extract from its own soil the produce with which to feed and clothe its people and at the same time lacks goods or commodities with which to buy from without the essentials for feeding and clothing its people. This is to say that primitive lands or even technologically backward countries such as China and India may be over-populated, but not such countries as have entered the system of machine industrialization and are or can be in the world market. Countries in the latter category which lack "living space" are suffering from defective social arrangements, not excess of population. In the case of Japan it cannot be denied that the country's economic basis is insecure, but the explanation lies not in the ratio of persons to area but rather to impediments to the most effective use of those resources. For some of these impediments Japan is itself to blame; for others it is not. But none of them is irremovable.

However, with all the false accentuations and disingenuous apologetics stripped off, Japan's economic problem must be taken into account. Japan must be allowed and helped to find a secure basis for its economy. Just curbing Japan in aggression is not enough. It will break bounds again and have to be curbed again unless within the limits to which it is confined its people can find a way of life that satisfies their needs. But in this there is nothing mystical or unique or calling for political arrangements or consequences peculiar to the Far East. There is nothing calling for a redrawing of territorial boundaries. What, then, is Japan's economic situation and in what way must cognizance be taken of it in arriving at a settlement in the Far East?

There are two fundamental facts that condition the social state of Japan. The first is that it has a population which has more than doubled in sixty years and now numbers some 70,000,000, pent within an area of less than 150,000 square miles of which only one-fifth is arable. The second is that Japan lacks most of the raw materials essential to industrial production. In result Japan admittedly has more people within its borders than can possibly be maintained on the resources of Japan proper. But one modifying fact must also be observed. Simultaneously with the increase in population there has been a rise in standard of living. There are too many mouths to feed, no doubt; but each has more to eat than before there were too many. So far from the increase in population causing a decline in standard of living, it may be said that the rise in standard of living has caused the increase in population. At least there is clear evidence of profound changes in amelioration at work in Japan, generated from within Japan itself as part of its development and wholly unrelated to any actions by the country outside its borders. For the rise in standard of living, coincident with the increase in population and despite the increase, had set in before Japan set out on a career of expansion presumably to find room for its excess population.

In other words, industrialization has had the same effect in Japan as everywhere else—increase of productivity and simultaneous increase of population, the curve of the latter first rising steeply and then tending to level off. For reasons growing out of Japan's geographical limitations it has been harder to arrive at a balance there than elsewhere, but the movement toward equilibrium is unmistakable. In the interim of disequilibrium resulting from the retarded tempo there must be serious dislocations and pressures creating their own explosive force. They must be relieved and the rest of the world must resign itself to whatever is required to provide relief. But it is clear, too, that Japan's real difficulties are more complex than is conveyed by demographic explanations, and their solution is not to be found in anything so simple as "outlets" for surplus population. It is highly doubtful that acquisition of more territory would provide a lasting remedy, if remedy at all. For equivalent to the gains from acquisition of territory might be the costs of acquiring and maintaining it.

Japan's difficulties are not demographic. They are of the time, characteristic of all countries that are in the social setting of the time. They have unique complexities and perhaps distinctive aggravations because of the circumstances in which Japan incorporated itself into the time, but they are not peculiarly Japanese nevertheless. The leitmotiv of nearly all writing on Japan for decades has been a note of breathless wonder at the "miracle" of Japan's transformation into a modern state in fifty years. Like all miracles, this one has always been subject to cold internal criticism. In the past it has been fair to question whether there was a transformation or just the superimposition of a new exterior. Railways, telegraphs, an effective navy and textile mills do not constitute a modern society. Until very recently Japanese institutions had changed but little in reality. They remained the institutions of a peasant-handicraft society with special modifications deriving from Japanese feudalism, and to them were attached the accouterments of the West. These were adjuncts to Japan, however, not an integral part of Japan. Or it might be said that Japan had donned an extra outer garment, but the body and spirit remained the body and spirit of Japan. The rest of the world, however, saw only the outer garment and was dazzled.

There are still questions to be put against Japan's transformation but they are different questions now. Now they are questions not as to fact but as to effect. In recent years the transformation has gone under the surface. Now Japanese institutions really have changed or are changing. If they are not wholly the institutions of an industrialized society, they are equally far from the institutions of a peasant-handicraft society. Instead of being a peasant-handicraft society with Western adjuncts, Japan is now an industrialized society with survivals of peasant-handicraft institutions and feudal forms. The problems of Japanese government, business and finance essentially are the problems of Western government, business and finance.

Japan has performed its feat, a prodigious one if not miraculous, and now it is beginning to pay the price. The effects of industrialism are cumulative, and in Japan they have begun to tell. Until latterly Japan has had only the advantages of Westernism—wealth, power, extension of range, comfort and efficiency. It has begun now to get the disadvantages—dependence on foreign trade; dependence on external sources of raw materials; burden of armament expenditures to support expansionist policies based on need for foreign trade and foreign raw materials; entanglement in the world economy; wider diffusion of education resulting in internal discontent, though class antagonisms are as yet only incipient; submergence of the agrarian population. That Japan has succeeded in adapting Westernism can no longer be doubted. What can be doubted is whether it is any more successful in escaping the penalties of Westernism than the West has been. On the evidence thus far the answer is in the negative. Indeed, to the disabilities inherent in industrialism Japan has added incumbrances of its own making.

In a sense Japan succeeded all too well. Had its progress been more halting, even stumbling, so that it would have been necessary to retrace steps, Japan might have been a healthier country today. If it had taken a hundred years or even seventy-five years to do what it did in fifty, there would have been time to make an adjustment between the old and the new. The displacement of the old could have proceeded at equal pace with the advent of the new. Instead the new was just overlaid on the old. There was Osaka, and just outside Osaka there were peasants cultivating the soil as in the time of the Taira, but with one crucial difference—they were also living in a money economy. The old social organization, the old habits of thought, the old attitudes persisted. So, too, did the old perquisites of the small group that had always ruled Japan, but with one crucial difference—those perquisites had taken on a magnitude that gave the ruling groups range and power undreamed of before, range and power as great as any ruling group has ever had anywhere. A military feudal oligarchy became a capitalistic feudal oligarchy. The modulations that accompanied the development of industrialism and capitalism in the West, modulations which expressed the egalitarianism of the eighteenth century and the humanitarianism of the nineteenth, were lacking. Instead there was only a concentration of power, exercising unquestioned command of instruments for creating wealth but also exercising the prerogatives of an older social order. The forms of modern constitutional government were façade; behind them there was a small minority, for practical purposes absolute, and a mass which was inert, voiceless, exploited and content.

The mass was content because it had known nothing else and had gone through no experience from which it could perceive that there was anything else. There was no slow but sure induction into concepts of rights such as had preceded the coming of the industrial revolution in the West and precluded the perpetuation of its worst abuses. There was only a sudden change of name for the principle on which distribution of power was determined. Indeed, it may be said that the authority of the minority was reinforced by the Restoration, even though the goal of the Restoration was modernism. It is for this reason that the feudal spirit, if not the feudal forms, survived in Japan and co-exists with rapid transit, mass production and experimental science. Officially feudalism was abolished, but not the unquestioning loyalty which is its essence. Habits formed under certain institutions will outlive the institutions among any people; but in Japan it was skillfully contrived that they should do so. The emperor cult is in reality a coalescence of localized loyalties and their transference to a single object. Because of the sharpness of the transition from the old order to the new the quality of the loyalty was unchanged; or, if anything, it was more firmly fixed.

In the centuries of feudalism before the Restoration loyalty was the distinguishing mark of the warrior caste, the obligation of the samurai to his daimyo. It was thus a mark of superiority. The peasant was submissive rather than loyal. His was the obedience of a lower order rather than the obedience of a code. It was negative, as the peasant was negative. A change was beginning to manifest itself, however, toward the end of the Tokugawa Shogunate. The traditions of military feudalism were already relaxing. In part, the reason lay in the long internal peace imposed by the Tokugawas and the seclusion which shut out any external perils. In larger part, perhaps, the reason lay in the emergence of a merchant class, as in Europe in the Middle Ages. With the overthrow of the Shogunate following America's forcible intrusion, the restoration of the Emperor and the abolition of feudalism, there was the danger which confronts any society in the interregnum between one system and another. It was to the credit of the men who guided the country through its transition that they perceived the danger of a vacuum, the danger that lay in the breakdown of one set of traditions and values without the substitution of another.

The emperor cult was the solution. The emperor became the new focal point of the loyalties once devoted to numerous nobles. But now loyalty was no longer a privilege of the superior caste. It could be exercised, in fact it had to be exercised, by everybody. The emperor cult was a leveler. To most of the race it represents a step upward in the human scale, an admission into the comity of the nation. In the same way the extension of the right to bear arms from the samurai to the whole nation through conscription acted as leveler and signified for the mass a step upward in the human scale. To individuals of the mass it gave a social dignity and a sense of human worth they had never possessed before. It is inherent in the Japanese scheme, therefore, that the symbol of the emperor should have the force that it has and that military worship should be as binding as it is. The hold of the army on Japanese sentiment is easy to understand. It is also inherent in the Japanese scheme that authority should be unchallenged, that the majority should be submissive, and that the minority should have the advantage both of the prerogatives of a simpler social structure and the power that comes from the wealth that industrial production makes possible.

The industrialization of Japan was parcelled out to the great clans after the manner of concessions or franchises. This was not so much deliberate as in the natural course, which is in itself indicative. The decision to make Japan a modern state and society was handed down from above and executed from above, the tasks being delegated to those who always had had power and the rewards being allotted to them. The landed families became the industrial and financial families; it is true that as the nineteenth century wore on and the industrial structure broadened, the base, too, had to be broadened, and new groups attached themselves to the original nucleus, being as it were coopted. But the principle of an apex of wealth and power remained.

There was a kind of transposition of tokens of wealth and power from land and retainers to bonds and shares in quasi-official monopolies and corporations. And as industrialization proceeded and Japan came nearer to being counted as modern in productive apparatus, the center of gravity rose and the economy of the country became top-heavy.

An economy, like any other body, is unstable when top-heavy. Here lies Japan's weakness, rather than in its surplus population. Nearly half the population is still engaged in agriculture—within the money economy but not yet of it. The agrarian population must carry the high overhead of an industrial country in the form of its share of taxes for public services, a widely ramifying administration, a military establishment. In many respects, such as the provision of schools, highways, electric lights and other public utilities, it enjoys a standard of living not consonant with subsistence farming. But the proportion of income which must go to sustain these cannot be met out of the rewards of small-scale, hand-labor subsistence farming. Agrarian Japan is unhealthy, with a malady which spreads infection through the whole social system. It keeps alive by a kind of cupping—its young being drawn off into the reservoirs of cheap labor in factory towns. And so long as these reservoirs can be filled from the farms, factory wages will remain low, also at subsistence level. Thus, one-half of Japan lives in the social framework of the twentieth century, the other half in the eighteenth or early nineteenth at the latest. Except for purposes of production more than one-half of the population must be counted out of the economy, hence

Japan's abnormal dependence on foreign trade. At the best, Japan's position would be difficult because of the necessity of importing raw materials. The difficulty is aggravated because its economic organization does not permit the larger part of the population to absorb the product of industry. In a word, neither the agrarian nor the urban masses have income enough to buy enough of the country's production for the country to be sound. And the correctives found elsewhere in the form of active organization and positive demands by the underprivileged through political channels and by labor organization are lacking, because authority is still strongly entrenched and the habit of obedience or rather of passive resignation is still too deeply ingrained.

In this way the disabilities inherent in the industrial system press on Japan more than elsewhere. Furthermore, as has been said, Japan has added incumbrances of its own making. By this is meant the insensate chauvinism and aggressive expansionism that have characterized it since the Russo-Japanese war and that were present in germ almost as soon as the Restoration had consolidated itself. Indeed, if one knew nothing of the social history of the Western world in the last generation one might conclude that Japan's troubles are wholly attributable to the frenzied attempt to annex the Far East. As has been said, the larger phenomena evident in Japan are common to the whole industrialized world, but in their immediate, critical aspect they are the difficulties not of an industrial, capitalistic economy but of a war economy. In fact, one might make a strong case in refutation of economic determinism from the evidence of Japan.

Had Japan not surrendered to a heedless career of conquest, it would in all likelihood be sounder today than any other country numbered among the modern and great. Ten years ago it had just come into the stage of industrial effectiveness. It had for the first time arrived at a position of active competition for world trade, the position from which it has made such successful inroads into the markets of almost every other country in every other part of the world. Had Japan confined its expansion within those limits it might now have been stable and, compared with the rest of the world, prosperous. Out of the profits of an increasing trade it could have accumulated a surplus with which to finance the extension of productive facilities into heavy industry, thus progressively lessening its dependence on the West. Out of the profits of an increasing trade there could have been paid a progressively wider margin of real wages, thus redounding proportionately to the prosperity of industry. Thus Japan might have strengthened its foundation. Japan did, as a matter of fact, escape the worst impacts of the world depression; it might also have fortified itself. Though Japan might have been caught in "the internal contradictions" of the system together with all other countries in the system, it might have been able to postpone constriction. Instead, Japan is perhaps in as bad a case as any European country now being bled by the war. In fact, until the European war broke out Japan was probably in a worse case than most countries in Europe.

To be sure, nationalism and expansion are inseparable from industrialism, are part of the social setting into which Japan has merged itself. They may even flow from modern industrialism. To a degree Japan's attempts to conquer the Far East followed from its success in reaching the stage of industrial effectiveness. That is to say, it had come to a point where it had to have access to the raw materials to be found on the Asiatic continent and outlet for its products. Even in its most egregious form Japanese lust for conquest has a certain economic motivation. The fear that other empires would preempt the mainland and close the door to Japan economically, thus forever stunting Japan's economic growth, had a share in prompting aggression. But it is clear that guarding against this danger did not require Japan to go to the lengths that it has, and that an uncontrolled militarism, uncontrolled because Japan in spirit still dwells in a feudal age, is more nearly responsible for Japan's precarious position. Negative measures in restraint of other empires would have sufficed. Japan was strong enough to proclaim and enforce a genuine Monroe Doctrine, an injunction against further Western penetration. It might have gone further and assisted China in recovering independence, thus winning a kind of moral priority on the continent. The economic motive enters into Japan's imperialistic career, but the economic motive with a peculiar and wilful twist.

What, then, can be done to satisfy Japan's economic needs, thus depriving it of legitimate grounds for seeking to extend its boundaries by force as a means of self-preservation, of livelihood? From what has just been said it follows that Japan must be freed from political fears, from fears that it will be pent within its islands by the aggressions of other Powers. This is to say that there must be a genuine Monroe Doctrine for East Asia—an acknowledgment by all Powers that the Far East is no longer subject to colonization by the West, with the corollary, expressed or implicit, that the Doctrine is simultaneously a self-denying ordinance on Japan's part. In other words, Japan will have the right as the strongest Power in the East to act in case of any attempt by a Western Power to extend its sway in the Far East. In this connection, parenthetically, Russia must be classified as a Western Power. As has been said in an earlier chapter, there must begin at the same time the withdrawal of Western Powers from China, in stages rather than precipitately, but unmistakable withdrawal nevertheless. And a beginning must be made toward relaxation of Western control over other possessions in Eastern waters, to the end of preparing the inhabitants of those possessions for induction into the exercise of full sovereign rights. It must be possible to foresee the time, at no distant date, when the Western Powers will withdraw from the Far East entirely, not in favor of other Powers not now possessing colonies but in favor of the inhabitants of what are now colonies. If this be a sacrifice then it is one which is in the movement of history in any case. Not only in China but elsewhere in the East native nationalisms will not long be denied. Empires will have to fight to prolong their hold or withdraw sooner or later, and probably have to withdraw even if they do fight. If, then, the inevitable is anticipated in order to give Japan a sense of security which might make it willing to renounce aggression, the price is not exorbitant.

Politically this is all that is required to give Japan economic assurance. It is as much as Japan can win for itself by political measures for economic purposes. Conquest will not solve Japan's problem of feeding a growing population. For that Japan is not strong enough. It has neither the man-power nor the resources nor the industrial establishment to hold China in subjection and at the same time withstand rival empires, whether the older empires it has dispossessed or the new fascist empires just setting out on aggrandizement—to say nothing of Russia, whether fascist or communist. Nor has it the means of developing the areas it aspires to conquer. No matter how rich those areas are in the natural resources that Japan covets, Japan is too poor to extract them. China and the Netherlands Indies may be an El Dorado under the surface, but their riches will remain under the soil until there is an enormous expenditure of capital to bring them out. And there must be a long interval between the time that the capital is expended and the time that profits can be reaped. Just transportation facilities and plant alone, to say nothing of the whole complex overhead of modern industrial enterprise, is prodigiously costly. And until transportation facilities and plant are established, there is no return on capital invested, for the capital cannot start working. In the interval the capital must be written off. In other words, the capital must come from a country with a surplus of liquid capital so large that it can sequester a considerable proportion in the expectation of large future returns.

All colonial experience proves that the success or failure of any colonial acquisition depends less on the intrinsic worth of the colony than on the wealth of the colonizing country. A country rich enough to pour capital into a colony in order to develop its resources, rich enough to wait until the resources begin to pay and rich enough at the same time to fortify itself against other countries that resent its acquisition, can make a colony profitable. No other country can, no matter what the colony is. Japan cannot. It is not rich enough. It has not been industrialized long enough to have accumulated a large surplus of mobile capital. Manchukuo alone imposed a severe strain, and since then there has been a war which has all but drained the country. If Japan had the assets of the United States or Great Britain, it might be able to realize its imperialistic aspirations; but it has not. So far from winning sustenance for a growing population by an attempt to maintain imperial grandeur, Japan is more likely to draw off its life-blood and weaken its fibers, making itself ready for the kill by more powerful rivals.

What is called Japan's population problem is at bottom a product of Japan's industrialization, since to industrialization may be attributed the increase in numbers which has created the problem. And by further industrialization alone can the problem be solved. Neither conquest nor emigration can provide a solution. Time will help, in the sense that with the passage of time the rate of increase will decline. Increase of population has been an inseparable accompaniment of industrialization everywhere; so apparently is a declining rate of increase until there is quantitative stabilization. In Japan the latter movement has already set in, and it is generally agreed that the second half of the present century will not be far advanced before Japan's population has reached its peak. The intervening years will be no more difficult than the last thirty, say; less so, in all probability, since Japan's industrial productivity is higher. And for a numerically static nation the solution is by way of industrialization. By industrialization Japan can produce that with which it can procure food and other necessaries for its people.

There are two requisites for Japan's successful industrialization: opportunity to purchase raw materials, outlet for manufactured products. Both Japan must have in order to exist; for both it will fight; to ensure those it is justified in fighting. But to ensure them Japan is not required to fight or even to expand. In fact, not only is Japan not unfavorably situated with regard to both, but it actually has advantages. It lies at the door of a continent which offers both natural resources and raw materials. It has competitive advantages of propinquity and cultural kinship, for all other industrialized countries and prospective countries are distant and racially and culturally alien. By normal economic processes Japan can buy the raw materials of the Asiatic mainland and sell finished products to the Asiatic mainland. In the working of normal economic processes it can buy the raw materials cheaper, since its transportation costs are lower, and sell goods back cheaper, since its transportation costs are lower. Nothing can prevent Japan from getting the larger share of the continent's raw materials and the larger share of the continental market except political impediments, and in the last thirty years these have been wholly of Japan's making. No other Power has been in a position to appropriate to itself the trade of China or by threat of force hope to exclude Japan. Insofar as Japan's opportunities have been restricted, it is because of the antagonism aroused in China by Japanese aggressions.

China is Japan's natural economic sphere for at least a generation, and by the opportunities to be found in that sphere Japan can keep itself not only solvent but moving on a rising scale of wealth and standard of living. As has already been explained, the industrial development of China can sustain the industrially advanced countries for years. Japan has by no means exhausted the potentialities of the China market for cheap consumers' goods. This market is almost exclusively Japan's, since it does not pay to transport very cheap commodities from Europe or America. And beyond that lies the real opportunity—that of supplying China's needs for capital and producers' goods over the decades in which China is itself industrializing. And while this is not exclusively Japan's market, Japan must get the larger share. But China must be left at peace so that it can proceed with reconstruction, and it must not be so embittered that it will operate what is almost a regime of non-intercourse with Japan except in what is absolutely essential. At the best, so long as China is fearful and therefore hostile, China's market for loans is closed to Japan. Under harmonious relations China could absorb the whole of Japanese surplus capital in loans for its own reconstruction. In return Japan could get raw materials. As the purchasing power of China was increased by the reconstruction paid for by Japanese loans and more of the country was opened up to foreign trade, Japan would prosper in proportion, selling first consumers' goods and then more producers' goods. The excess mouths of Japan could be fed from China—without sending them to China, or even better at home than if they were sent to China.

It goes without saying that no other Power must seek to interpose obstacles to this process, and it is obvious that no other Power is in a position to do so unless it be Russia. But Russia's strength in China has been made by other Powers, which is to say, by China's resentment against other Powers and China's belief that Russia may be of assistance in throwing off their encroachments. Russia can establish itself in China in such a position as to bar out Japan or deflect reconstruction only if Japanese attacks so undermine China's strength that China is helpless or China invites Russia to enter as being less disagreeable than Japan. The Monroe Doctrine of Eastern Asia of which the Japanese have talked so insistently in recent years is in its essence almost a natural endowment of the region, an expression of geography. Only Japan can prevent its application in essentials and in such a way as to offer Japan national prosperity and solution of its social problems; and thus far Japan has succeeded in doing so.

China is Japan's natural sphere, but the area of Japanese economic activity cannot be rigidly demarcated by China's boundaries. As it is necessary to begin a progressive relaxation of political control over Western dependencies in Eastern waters, so too it is necessary to begin a progressive relaxation of economic control in Japan's favor. It is necessary to extend most-favored nation treatment to Japan or at least in stages to dismantle the tariff barriers that have been raised against Japan to save the trade of the dependencies for the respective empires. The result will be the ultimate displacement of the metropolitan countries in the markets of their own colonial possessions, but this, too, is in the movement of history and is, moreover, ordained by geography. Only superior military force or the threat thereof can keep Eastern lands in the Western orbit politically and especially economically, once there is a single Eastern country that is physically strong and economically efficient. Only superior military power, in other words, can withstand the natural force of time and place. The economic rewards of the Far East must go to Japan, since Japan is of the Far East and is economically advanced. They will continue to go to Japan so long as it is the only Far Eastern land to be industrialized. In effect, this means Japan will get first access to the raw materials of the lands of the Far East and the larger share of the market of those lands. It will get them without the "manifest destinies" in the minds of its army philosophers or the "southward drives" of its navy philosophers. It will get them without imperialistic conquest on the pattern of the nineteenth century, and in so doing is secure in its place in the world, secure in its own economic and social system.

These are not movements in a social vacuum, however. They entail sacrifices on the part of Western Powers—sacrifices of trade they now have and, still more, of potential trade they had counted on, trade in continuously increasing quantity and value as throughout the nineteenth century. These are sacrifices not willingly borne at any time and not easily borne now, when the economic plight of Western countries is as it is. But they must be made willingly if there is to be peace in the Far East, if, that is, Japan is to refrain from aggression; as to whether they can be borne, that is subordinate to the larger question of the economic evolution of the Western world in the near future. Renunciation of economic monopoly in the East need not necessarily mean an absolute reduction of returns from the East. Indirect returns from economic development may balance the loss from monopoly. Whether the functioning of the present economic system requires continuous expansion of opportunity and extension of market cannot be established beyond dispute. If it does, then the sacrifices that are called for to ensure a lasting peace in the Far East will impose the necessity either of economic decline for the West or a reshaping of its economic institutions. But this question is internal to the West and must be settled in the West. It is generically the question that is put by all other international situations, by international relations as a whole. It will have to be settled with reference not alone to the Far East. All that need be said on that question here is that it may be that for reasons innate in the economic system the choice lies between chronic war in the Far East and economic reorganization in the West. If so, then the West will choose according to which it fears more, or, rather, which it prefers—the existing economic system with war or peace at the price of another economic system.

It is also possible that there may be another economic

system without assurance of peace and without peace as a conscious end. Under an international system consisting of regional totalitarian blocs the elements of the international economic problem may be so different or so differently combined that no analysis made now is valid; but it is difficult to see on what formula they can be combined in such a way as to circumvent principles. Even as between totalitarian blocs there will be allocation of the Eastern regional bloc to Japan— to the extent at least that that bloc will move in a Japanese orbit—or there will be conflict. Totalitarian organization may absolve the Western economic systems from dependence on economic returns from the East altogether; but as has been said in another connection, that cannot be determined until it is revealed in the event whether totalitarianism is a transitory phenomenon of a socially diseased period or is in the line of social evolution.

So far as questions local to the Far East are concerned it is clear in which direction lies solution for Japan without military aggression and therefore extrication of the Far East from the war system. In more intensive industrialization, through unimpeded access to continental raw materials and continental markets, Japan has scope for its economy and sustenance for its population; but not in that alone. There are questions internal to Japan, too, questions generically of the same order as those that confront the West. Japan cannot exist half-mechanized, half-feudal. It cannot on its upper layers function as the Ruhr, Lancashire, Detroit, and at its base as a system of contiguous mediaeval villages. Nor can it keep a highly productive apparatus occupied in exports alone. Japan's weakness now lies in its abnormal dependence on foreign trade. This is a consequence not so much of its geographical deprivations as of the disinheriting of the mass of its people, rather of their exclusion from economic life. In other words, there is necessary, too, a redistribution of income within Japan. The peasant cannot be kept on a subsistence level and the worker on the wage level of the handicraft artisan. Economically the lower classes must be permitted to rise in the social scale. In short, there must be social reorganization within Japan as well as economic opportunity outside Japan, if Japan is to rest on a solid foundation, with or without imperialistic glories, with or without economic opportunities on the Asiatic continent by reason of Western renunciation and Chinese conciliation. For Japan's population problem, that which presumably motivates its political conduct, is social as much as biological, internal as much as external.

Beyond that Japan's future is as the future of the West, as its fundamental problems are in essence indistinguishable from those of the West. Production and distribution of goods by machinery will not exempt Japan from internal difficulties, as it has not exempted the West. It will allay some difficulties and raise others equally serious. But these are not distinctively Japanese difficulties; they are common to all of the world embraced in the industrial revolution. Whatever the evolution of industrial, nationalistic, capitalistic society holds for the West it holds for Japan too. What that is can hardly be even conjectured, especially in 1940. But having thrown itself into the stream of Western civilization in the nineteenth century, Japan must be carried along with it.

CHAPTER VI

THE INTERNAL NEEDS OF CHINA

Defeated or victorious, China will nevertheless remain the center of gravity in the Far East, as it always has been. According as there is equilibrium in China's relations with the rest of the Far East will there be equilibrium in the Far East. According as there is stability within China will there be stability in the Far East. By reason of its area, population and resources China will remain determinant for the Far East. If for example Japan does wield supremacy in Asia it will do so by virtue of its possession of China, and such weight and influence as it exerts in world politics will derive from its control over China. China will continue to give direction to the course of international relations in Asia, but the direction will be fixed as much by the internal state of China as by its external relations. It is necessary, therefore, in any inquiry into the conditions of peace in the Far East to take account of China's internal problems. China's needs as well as Japan's must be satisfied if there is to be peace.

Much of what is pertinent in this connection has already been discussed in earlier chapters. To a great extent what was said of China's foreign relations applies equally to its domestic problems. In domestic as well as foreign affairs the prime essential for China is recovery of freedom of action, and this can come about only by the restoration of independence. China is a country of continental dimensions in a state of social and cultural disintegration produced by the disruptive effects of the thrusts of a more vigorous culture. Its fundamental problem is to make a transition to a new society and culture more consonant with the forces of the time. But this it cannot do under duress and continuously compelled to ward off threats. It cannot concentrate the greater part of its energies and resources on efforts for self-preservation and at the same time have enough of either for building railways, opening schools to eliminate illiteracy, establishing national currencies and banking systems, instituting public services of all kinds—in short, laying the foundations for the whole complex and costly apparatus of a modern state and economy.

China, too, has a population problem. It has been lost sight of in all the polemics over Japanese population pressure, but in actuality China is further from being able to feed its people than Japan. Given the present number of human beings within the territorial bounds of China, the rate of increase and the country's capacity to produce with existing methods of production, it would be physically impossible for China to carry on except by the operations of the Malthusian law. There must be floods, droughts, famines, plagues and wars to drain off the excess for the rest to survive. The Malthusian law does operate, but even so a large proportion of the population is barely kept alive; it subsists, but no more. As with Japan, neither emigration nor conquest offers a solution; millions of Chinese have already emigrated without any appreciable effect. Relief can come about in two ways only: reduction of population by birth control or by what can be called the reflex action of a rising standard of living, as in all countries which have industrialized, and industrialization itself to increase productivity. China, too, must industrialize. It must do so because only thereby can any country acquire the means of defense indispensable to survival in our time and because only thereby can it support its people.

Industrialism, however, entails more than volition and choice. It requires a new social foundation, a new structure of harmonious institutions. And these require time, capital, freedom from other demands on wealth, immunity from attack or threat of attack. Foreign intrusion cuts fissures in any nation. It prevents both moral and physical unity. The foreign issue crosses and obscures all other issues. It can be made use of by the unscrupulous. It gives scope to venality: certain groups can always be induced to serve the intruder at a price. And a country rent within cannot undertake reconstruction. It has neither the freedom of mind, nor the security requisite to planning with perspective and executing with efficiency. It must devote itself wholly to circumventing further alien penetration. Nor can it call on all its potential wealth. For it is that which is most valuable that is preempted by foreign intruders or sought by those who attempt intrusion. Had China been able to put to constructive use the wealth consumed in the years between 1920 and 1940 to regain independence or fight off invasion, the country would now have been far along on the path to modernization and social effectiveness by the standards of our time. But it will never get far on that path until it is wholly free from the necessity of repelling attack. In this sense every domestic question down to the most narrow local issue has some foreign aspect, is in some measure involved with international relations.

Complete independence with reasonable security is a condition precedent to social reconstruction. National unification is another. The internecine struggles that have broken out intermittently since 1911 have been an obstacle less serious only than foreign incursion. If continued, they would be enough to negate any hope of reconstruction even if there were complete freedom from foreign attack. It hardly needs to be pointed out that disunity is an effect as well as a cause, that it is a product of the same conditions that demand reconstruction. For indispensable to effective unification is the physical integration of the country by adequate communications. There is something of a circle here: effective unification is difficult until there is reconstruction, and reconstruction is difficult until there is effective unification. But in the order of dependence unification is easier to attain first, as is evidenced by the progress that was being made in that direction before 1937. And the progress made since then has been impressive. Indeed, it may be that Japan is doing for China what China could not do for itself. It is instilling forces of cohesion that China could not generate from within and that really bind the country. And from all the evidence of the war years it may be anticipated that failing the interjection of new factors China will be a united country if it escapes the Japanese onslaught.

If there is independence and unification, then next in order of importance is assistance from abroad—financial and technical assistance. Industrialization and modernization are impossible of attainment anywhere without great reserves of liquid capital on which to draw. It need not be pointed out that no unindustrialized country has such reserves. Unless therefore a country is to wait for the slow accumulation of surplus from development by its own slender capital resources, a period which may extend over generations, it must have access to foreign capital. For self-evident reasons China cannot wait. It must borrow. It must receive loans from abroad. Furthermore, unless a country without any background or experience in modern technology is to wait for decades while its own schools can train scientists, engineers and mechanics it must be able to draw on foreign technical skill. But with respect to foreign loans and foreign technicians alike, there must be sure safeguards against political accompaniments. In other words, loans must be purely financial transactions, being made on ordinary commercial security or the general credit of the country. There can be no more supervision or control of Chinese public services, public utilities or administrative organs as a measure of security on the model of the past. Otherwise there will be the negation of Chinese sovereignty and a resumption of the old order of international rivalry for preferred positions, with loans as the means of taking positions and control of administrative organs as the means of holding positions taken. Similarly, foreign technicians, whether managing directors of railways or chief foremen of factories, must be engaged as employes of China, subject to the authority of those who engage them, and not as "advisers" with quasi-independent and quasi-diplomatic status on the model of the past.

Otherwise there will also be the negation of Chinese sovereignty and a resumption of international intrigue for "adviserships" as vanguards of imperialistic advance. Under normal conditions of freedom from external attack and civil strife China's resources can offer sufficient security for foreign loans. The "productivity potential" from unimpeded industrial development is ample guaranty of capacity to repay.

Given independence, unification, foreign loans and foreign technical assistance, the conditions for successful industrialization will have been met. But successful industrialization alone is not a guaranty of internal stability. Social reconstruction in China calls for more than revolution in methods of production and increase in wealth. In China as in Japan a society cannot exist at odds within itself. China cannot live half in the Occidental twentieth century and half in the Oriental Middle Ages. It will solve nothing with respect to internal stability or equilibrium in Far Eastern international relations if great factory centers in Shanghai, Canton, Tientsin, Hankow and Chungking are superimposed on a substratum of peasants ground by rackrenting, usury and manipulation of crop prices and urban factory hands working fourteen hours a day at wages which barely keep them alive. A country which has become a gigantic sweatshop will not remain long at poise within, and even if it has an efficient, modern army and navy it will not long remain independent, for there will develop inner frictions which will lay it open to united enemies. The difficulties and dislocations of contemporary Japan will be reflected in China, but in much higher degree. For China begins its transformation already over-populated, as Japan did not. Also, there is no long heritage of feudalism to keep the Chinese submissive to authority. Unless pari passu with the increase of wealth from industrialism there is a rise in the level of the submerged classes, which now include most of the Chinese people, there will be, as in Japan, pressures that generate their own explosive force, but in China they will be more devastating. China will not find a temporary safety valve in easy external aggression, as Japan did. Japan had China to look to for outlet; China has not. Japan acquired modern armament when all the region around it was wholly unarmed; China starts when nearly all the surrounding peoples have already begun to arm. There cannot be the same technological disparity in its favor that Japan enjoyed. In China there can be only one vent for internal pressures—social upheaval. And social upheaval will re-start the whole sequence of events that constitutes Far Eastern history up to the present.

The touchstone is the agrarian problem, for not only does it concern nearly nine-tenths of the population but because there lies China's most serious weakness. Until it is solved China's situation must remain hopeless. No military victories, political reforms or industrial development will be of avail until the lot of the peasants is alleviated. Ad hoc measures of reform can provide some relief. The most flagrant abuses can be checked. Rents can be reduced by imposing legal limits and enforcing them. Usury can be abolished by the infliction of severe punishments. By rural credit banks and cooperative marketing the peasants' costs can be reduced and income increased. Exploitation of the peasants in market centers and by unscrupulous tax collectors can be stopped. These would all be of no little benefit to the peasant. They would ease his life considerably. But they touch only the surface of the problem.

Fundamentally there are too many people on the land, given the existing methods of tilling the soil—the methods, that is, by which the soil was tilled by all races until the advance of science had put the knowledge of plant and animal biology, soil chemistry and machine implements at the service of the farmer. The products of the soil could be multiplied manifold, of course, by reclamation, re-afforestation, irrigation and better selection of seeds and domestic animal breeds; but like modern armament these cannot be invoked by will or brought about in themselves. They are the products of a system—of the industrial system, of a society in which the application of science has created new ways of dealing with the environment, new attitudes, a new way of life. No one part of that system can be taken by itself. All parts are inseparable from each other and from the whole. There must be literacy and technical schools and laboratories and trained technicians before there can be either machine guns and bombing planes or cheap fertilizers and seed corn selected by cross-breeding to yield twice as many ears.

Increase of the productivity of the soil would sustain more people on the land; but it is fairly certain that there would still be more than could be properly nourished except insofar as the application of science to production generally drew a proportion of the rural population off into the cities to work in factories. Here again there is the interaction of industrialization and agrarian reform. There is interaction also with respect to the principles that will underlie and guide reconstruction both on the land and in the city. If the surplus population on the land is to be taken only as a reservoir of cheap labor for the city, then neither the rural nor urban population is much better off. Nor is the agrarian economy much better off. The urban population will be unable to buy much of the increased produce of the land. The peasant will be living on a money economy without much cash. He will benefit only to the extent that there will be more grain to feed fewer mouths. As in Japan he will have to pay more taxes to support the expensive public services and administrative organism of an industrialized society without any appreciable increase in real income; he will be permanently in debt, like the Japanese peasant. And since he will have no cash margin with which to buy the increased production of the machine in the cities, the factories will have to dump abroad and keep the wage level as low as possible without causing actual starvation. All that will have been accomplished, then, is that fewer persons will die of malnutrition than now both in the city and country; but the whole economy and social system will be as unworkable as now. They will be even more unworkable than now, in fact. For through the centuries a certain balance has been struck which keeps China at even keel most of the time—with periodic seismic upheavals when it fails to do so, a kind of cycle of internal peace and civil war. But industrialism and partial agrarian reform on the old principles of dividing the rewards of labor will add Western mal-adjustments to those endemic to the native system.

Industrialism is prerequisite to stability in China and peace in the Far East, but it will contribute to neither if it is carried out in such a way as to reproduce the evils of the earlier phases of industrialism in the West and in Japan. Then indeed there will be only a gigantic sweatshop—worse even than early nineteenth century Europe at its worst, for there will not be the restraints of the egalitarianism that preceded indus-trialism and the humanitarianism that accompanied or closely followed it. The lack of any concept of individ-ualism and individual rights was no serious handicap in China when there was effective clan organization; in an industrial society it would be fatal. The result would be the worst helotry the world has known and, later, the bloodiest revolution the world has known.

There must be reconstruction in China, but it must be social as well as material reconstruction. It must be reconstruction not at the point at which Europe began more than a century ago but at the point at which the West now finds itself. In other words, there must be social reconstruction infused with a new social philos-ophy, one which applies the lessons of Western experi-ence in the last hundred years—or, rather, in the last ten years. The test is the distribution of income, and this will be both determined and revealed by the de-gree of social control that is applied to the process of industrialization and its results. If there is complete laissez faire and favored groups or those which com-mand enough capital to come in on the ground floor are allowed to proceed with industrialization without

restriction and with unimpeded access to natural resources, a course will be laid which leads to chronic
turmoil within China and strife without. This can be
avoided and, instead, a foundation laid for a stable system if the principle of control is established and actual
control exercised. Both tendencies have already manifested themselves in China. The earlier developments
in Shanghai and elsewhere in the Yangtze Valley have
had all the stigmata of what is worst in the West, mixed
with what is worst in the old East. And some of the
characteristics of the dominant financial groups in
Shanghai and environs are disquieting in what they
portend. Yet there have been at the same time indica-
tions of awareness of dangers and the determination
to avoid them. A nation not indoctrinated with the
sanctity of laissez faire does not construe as blasphemous
the placing of restrictions by government on the pri-
vate exploitation of natural resources. The doctrine of
Sun Yat-sen's San Min Chu I, which with all its internal vagaries and contradictions was a statement of
the philosophy of social control, has prepared the nation for acceptance of restrictions on economic freedom in the general interest. Whether the earlier spirit
of Sun Yat-sen prevails or the Sun Yat-sen doctrine is
taken in the letter and the spirit is that of the Shanghai bankers and industrialists, it is too early to say.
Whether either gives form and content to the social
structure of China depends first of all, of course, on
China's escaping subjection to Japan. But if China
does escape, it is the spirit of Sun Yat-sen that must pre-
vail or it will have served China very little to have

escaped Japan and it will have served the cause of peace in the Far East very little that Japan was frustrated.

Here again the element of China's foreign relations and political status enters. For China's choice even of internal social policy, of the larger principles that will determine its institutions, must be materially, if not crucially, affected by whether or not it is under threat of attack. In the period just preceding the war with Japan the necessity of preparing for that war could have been cited as an excuse for undermining the social safeguards laid down by Sun Yat-sen. The necessity of preparedness was as much a convenient excuse as a legitimate reason; but it cannot be disputed that had there been a sincere desire to maintain those safeguards, it would not have been possible to do so if there was to be adequate preparedness. When military roads must be built, arsenals equipped and set to working, reserves of raw materials, semi-manufactured goods and machines stocked, all in precipitate haste, it is not even advisable to maintain social safeguards which in their nature make production the secondary consideration. So, indeed, European countries have found in their war; indeed, it may be that Germany's sacrifice of all social consideration to manufacture of armament gave it the decisive advantage. Unless China can have a sense of security it cannot afford to retard the tempo of industrialization. It must give free rein to those who can produce most efficiently, without regard to ruinous exploitation of resources, cruelly long working hours and cruelly low wages. And restriction of profits, even restraints against profiteering, must be waived to ensure quick production. War or danger of war is always and everywhere the most effective saboteur of fundamental social reform and the most effective ally of the reactionary and the exploiter.

The price of social reform in an already established industrial society or of prevention of social abuses in a society newly industrializing is the retardation of development. The pace must be fixed not by the temptation of results but by the welfare of the majority. And social welfare and maximum production are nearly always mutually incompatible, if not mutually exclusive. Had it been possible in the West to foresee the deep-lying organic malformations and deformations that were being wrought in the course of the nineteenth century, it would still have been impossible to prevent them except at the price of retarding material progress. At the beginning of the twentieth century there would have been less wealth, less comfort, fewer roads and hospitals and universities and museums, not so much advance in the fight against disease. Social amelioration, whether by remedy or prevention, is an economic luxury. It can be afforded only by the secure. It cannot be afforded by China unless China does not have to have as quickly as possible a supply of modern arms—which is to say, a system of efficient factories—so that it can withstand attack by powerful empires aspiring to dominion over the Far East. If on the other hand China can feel assured of continued sovereignty and integrity it at least has the option of pacing its industrialization by considerations of the future health of the society. It is, in conclusion, far better for China to progress slowly in industrialization, but this it can do only if it is secure.

The necessity of social reconstruction in China has an urgency that derives from something more immediate than the comparative merits of social philosophies seen in perspective. Concrete circumstances will force China to certain choices. The social issue has already been put and will press for decision, with internal peace or war very likely hanging on the decision. There have been now fifteen years of social ferment, with the communist party as the leaven. In one sense the communist issue in China is factitious, even meretricious. Organized, official communist influence is no doubt artificial in origin, its growth and power deriving from external sources—first the refusal of Western empires to make concessions to China's aspirations for recovery of independence and then the Japanese invasion. But it would never have advanced very far had not conditions in China lent themselves to its appeal. For reasons inherent in China's place in the social scale, accentuated by the breakdown in recent years and the abuses of misgovernment, the suffering of the Chinese people had reached such a pitch that eruption of one kind or another was becoming almost a matter of physics, even if there had never been a revolution in Russia. The communist propaganda had material to work with, and the communist party has made the most of it. But if the communist party were to disappear now, scuttled by the U.S.S.R., there would be no subsidence of discontent in China. Suffering has not been diminished by the war with Japan; to the contrary, in China as elsewhere war has given forced growth to everything that was in the soil. With or without communist influence, if China remains a free agent there must be relief for the sufferings of the people, or there will be eruption.

There is communist influence, however, and it, too, has not been diminished by the war. To the contrary, the communists have exploited the opportunity created by the war. By the contribution they have made to resistance against the Japanese invaders they have enhanced their prestige and added to the number of their adherents. The contribution may have been exaggerated by communist sympathizers, especially in America; but it has been genuine and played no little part in cheating the Japanese of easy victory. Because of the communists' development of guerilla strategy and the intelligent use of mass education to lay a solid base for effective resistance, their influence has permeated far beyond what it could have, if there had been no war. And it has had something to work on—the material support which the Soviet Union has given China's cause.

If the war should end with Japan repelled, there will be a solid communist bloc, commanding influence, respect and the loyalty of large masses. And it is not to be expected that even if the communists have loyally joined in united resistance to the invader they have foresworn the desire to win control in the internal struggle. Unless, then, the present government of China has something to offer the people by way of concrete and thorough-going reforms to alleviate their suffering and thus counter the appeal of the communists, that appeal will not be withstood. It will win more adherents and gain force. As has already been said, there will be all the makings of another and more terrible

Spain—not only a civil war on social issues but a civil war with foreign allies for both sides. For if the Chinese communists make a bid for internal mastery, it is not to be expected that Soviet Russia will withhold support if it still has power to give support. And in that event it is not to be expected that the anti-communist Powers will not intervene to neutralize Russian support and prevent the creation of another soviet republic as a nominal partner in the Union of Soviet Socialist Republics. In that case, as has been said before, there will be not only another and more terrible Spain but the resumption of the old international struggle for power in Asia, with China as token in the struggle.

Social reconstruction in China, meaning industrialization and internal reorganization on a principle of economic equality, is a sine qua non of both internal equilibrium in China and international peace in the Far East.

POSTSCRIPT

A word of reservation is in order. For reasons having nothing to do with the Far East or the validity of the propositions herein developed, all that is submitted in this study may be no more than an intellectual exercise —an intellectual exercise in materials no longer of this world. The European war may negate all the premises here assumed and therefore make the conclusions irrelevant. With a fascist victory in Europe and Asia, all that is here proposed will have the effect and use of meditations in a dream world, of free speculation in a world created in fantasy. But whether or not the principles which have been stated as underlying a regime of international peace in the Far East can be applied now, they are the principles on which alone there can be peace in the Far East. If by reason of international developments elsewhere they belong in the realm of fantasy, that is only to say that for the present there will be no peace in the Far East. There will be at the best only fitful interludes between wars. If and when again the enterprise of making a civilized international order can be taken up, and another attempt made to subject national conduct to the jurisdiction of law binding on all nations—without which it is of course difficult to visualize permanent peace anywhere—it is submitted that the basis still will not have changed. In essence the problem will not have changed; the solution will be of the same order. Furthermore, it will be seen that the constituent elements of the problem are not exclusively Far Eastern; nor are the difficulties in the way of settlement innate to the Far East. The elements of the problem lie in the West as much as in the East. The difficulties derive from world conditions. Both problem and difficulties of solution lie in the nature of the social order founded on the revolution of science as applied to and manifested in the system of production and distribution of goods and the consequent incidence of the attributes of power. Both problem and difficulties will be affected as the nature of that order changes, moving in the direction which the course of its evolution takes. But in the first instance the problem will be given at least temporary formulation by the result of the European war and the difficulties will be magnified or reduced, perhaps raised to insuperability or eliminated altogether, according as that war ends and depending on the kind of world it produces.

INDEX

Agrarian problem, China, 104
  Japan, 80, 84
Anglo-Japanese alliance, 7
Anti-Comintern pact, 8
Asia, *see* Far East

Balance of power politics, 7, 64
Battle of the Concessions, 7
Boxer Rebellion, 8, 13

Canton, 24, 103
Capital goods, 46, 48
Capitalism, 22, 23, 33, 81
Central China Development Co., 57
China, 98 *ff.*
  agrarian problem, 104
  anti-foreignism, 22, 24
  anti-imperialism, 22, 24
  communist influence, 111-113
  communist movement, 25, 36
    defeat in 1927, 26
  defeat of Japan, 36, 52, 63
    effect on West, 39, 42, 43
  determinant for the Far East, 98
  distribution of income, 107
  economic needs, 99
    relations, 48
      with Japan, 49
    sphere for Japan, 92
  effect of the European War, 9, 64
    the World War, 14, 17
  extraterritoriality, 12, 18, 40, 63
  financial and technical assistance,
    101
  foreign concessions, 7, 12, 17, 18,
    40, 63
    market, 44
    privileges, 40
    relations, 12, 98, 109
  independence, 22, 24, 25, 34, 42,
    62, 63, 67, 70, 98

China—(*Continued*)
  industrialization, 42, 44, 53, 100,
    107
    in Manchuria, 29
    under Japanese domination,
      36, 37, 50, 51
  Japanese domination, 36, 37, 57
    argument for, 50
    effect on West, 37, 58
  Japanese puppet regimes, 30
  Kuomintang, 22, 27
  Kuomintang-U.S.S.R. agreement,
    22, 23
  modernization, 46, 53
    retarded by Japan, 53
  National Government at Nan-
    king, 29
    at Peking, 26
  Nationalism, 17, 19, 20, 22, 23, 33
  Nationalists, 22, 23, 24, 25, 27
  "New Order," 36, 68
  obligation to other Powers, 70
  opening of, 12, 14, 51
  partition of, 8
  "Planned" economy under Japan,
    37, 57
  political status, 109
  population problem, 76, 99
  purchasing power, 60
  railways in Manchuria, 28, 29
  raw materials, 57, 89
    for Japan, 57, 59
  reconstruction, 46, 53, 92, 100,
    107
  regional government in Manchu-
    ria, 28, 29
  revolution of 1911, 15, 17
  security from aggression, 109
  self preservation, 99
  social reconstruction, 100, 103,
    107, 110, 111, 113
  sovereignty, 7, 18, 67, 70

China—(*Continued*)
  territorial integrity, 7, 12, 17, 18
  treaty of 1842, 12
  treaty of 1860, 12
  treaty of Versailles, 17, 19
  tripartite bloc, 36, 57
  Twenty-One Demands, 14
  unequal treaties, 12, 17, 18, 41
  unification, 101
  U.S.S.R. aid, 71, 72, 112
    clash in Manchuria, 28
    domination by, 46, 73
  United States aid, 71, 74
  war with Japan, 3, 8, 29, 30, 46
    beginning of, 32
    causes of, 11
    defeat of Japanese, 36, 52, 62,
      63, 70
    effect on West, 39, 42, 43
  wars with England, 12
  Washington Conference, 18-21
  withdrawal of Western Powers,
    54, 67, 70, 88
Chinese Eastern R.R., 28
Chinese Nationalist Party, *see* Kuo-
  mintang
Chungking, 103
Coal, 57
Collective security, 71
Colonial uprisings, 16
Communications, development of,
  20
Communism, 25, 36
  in China, 111-113
Communist International, 22, 25
Concessions, in China, 7, 12, 17, 18,
  40, 63
Consumers' goods, 46, 47, 93
Cotton, 57
Credits, 46

Daimyo, 82

East Hopei puppet regime, 30
Economic determinism, 86
  system, free, 49, 55, 59
Emperor cult, 81, 82
Empires, 16, 22, 23
  relations between, 16
  relations with dependencies, 16

England, *see* Great Britain
Europe, balance of power, 7
  post-Napoleonic system, 6
  post-1918 system, 6
European war, 6, 114
  effect on the Far East, 9, 38, 64
Extraterritoriality, 12, 18, 40, 63

Far East, and European balance of
    power, 7, 13, 33
  and the U.S.S.R., 22, 73
  and the United States, 9, 14, 48,
    51, 65
  Anglo-Russian rivalry, 33
  British empire, 9, 39, 64, 66
  economic monopoly by the West,
    35, 94, 95
  effect of the European War, 9
  effect of the World War, 14
  French empire, 9, 39, 64, 66
  imperialist rivalries, 33
  international relations, 12
    and population problem, 75
  nationalism, 15, 20, 33, 88
  Netherlands empire, 9, 39, 89
  "New Order," 36, 68
  peace, conditions for, 62 *ff.*
  post-1842, 7
  post-1918, 7
  status quo, 9
  withdrawal of Western Powers,
    54, 67, 70, 88
Fascist victory, 9, 10, 114
Feudalism, 79, 80, 81, 82
Foreign concessions, 7, 12, 17, 18,
  40, 63
Free China, *see* China, independence
Free economic system, 49, 55, 59
France, 8
  empire in Far East, 9, 39, 64, 66

Germany, 6, 9, 10, 21, 39, 64, 73, 109
  and a Far East settlement, 65, 66
  economic relations, 48
  Nazi regime, 8
Great Britain, 8, 13, 33
  economic relations, 48
  empire in the Far East, 9, 39, 64,
    66

Hankow, 103
  British concession, 25

Imperialism, 22, 23, 41, 42
India, population problem, 76
Industrial system, cycle, 46-48
Industrialism, 33, 87
  and population problems, 76
  Western, 81, 107
Inner Mongolia, 30, 36
International peace, principles, 114
  in Far East, 114
International relations, 114
  and economic reorganization, 95
  and population problems, 75
  time factor, 21
Iron, 57
Italy, 8, 9, 64, 73
  and a Far East settlement, 65, 66

Japan, 75 ff.
  agrarian problem, 80, 84
  alliance with Britain, 7
  anti-communism, 36
  capitalistic feudal oligarchy, 80, 83
  chauvinism, 85
  conquest of Manchuria, 29, 30
  domination of China, 36, 37
    argument for, 50
    effect on West, 58
  domination of Far East, 36, 38
  economic exhaustion, 53, 62
    needs, 87
    problem, 76
    relations with China, 49
    sphere in China, 49, 92
  economy of, 84
  effect of the depression, 86
    the European war, 65
    the World War, 8, 14
  emperor cult, 81, 82
  Far East expansion, 34, 38, 64, 65, 66, 85, 86
  feudalism, 79, 80, 81, 82
  foreign market, 46
    policy, 69
  geographical limitations, 77
  in South Manchuria, 28, 29

Japan—(Continued)
  industrialization, 41, 45, 77, 90, 91
  industrialized society, 79
  insecurity, 68
  institutions, 78
  lack of raw materials, 77
  Manchukuo established, 30
  military feudal oligarchy, 80, 82
  military worship, 83
  most-favored-nation treatment, 94
  nationalism, 33, 86
  New Order in East Asia, 36, 68
  opening of, 82
  opposition to Western Powers, 69
  peasant-handicraft society, 78, 79
  political thought, 69
  population increase, 77
    problem, 75, 90
  rank as great power, 8
  Restoration, 81
  restraint of, 63
  social reorganization, 96
  "southward drive," 38
  standard of living, 77
  totalitarian, 61
  Twenty-One Demands, 14
  war economy, 86
  war with China, 3, 8, 29, 30, 46
    beginning of, 32
    causes of, 11
    defeat by China, 36, 52, 62, 63, 70
    effect on West, 39, 42, 43, 58
    victor over China, 36, 52, 53, 55, 62, 63
  war with Russia, 14
  westernized, 78, 80
  withdrawal of Western influence, 67
Japanese-German anti-Comintern pact, 8
Jehol, attack by Japan, 30

Konoye, Prince Fumimaro, 36
  New Order in East Asia, 36
Korea, 55

Kuomintang, 22, 27
  agreement with the U.S.S.R., 22,
    23
  program, 23

League of Nations, 30

Machinery, 49, 57
Malthusian theory, 75, 99
Manchu dynasty, 15, 17, 22
Manchukuo, 30, 32, 36, 37, 50, 53,
    55, 58, 90
Manchuria, 14, 28, 62
  conquest by Japan, 30
Marxism, 33
Mediterranean, 8
Military feudalism, 80, 82
Monroe Doctrine for East Asia, 68,
    88, 93
Most-favored-nation policy, 94
Multilateral trade, 48

Nanking, 29
Nationalism, 15, 20, 33, 88
Naval armaments limitation, 18
Netherlands, empire in Far East,
    9, 39
  raw materials, 89
New Order in East Asia, 36, 68
North China, 14, 36
  attack by Japan, 30
North China Development Co., 57
North China Political Council, 30
North Manchuria, 28, 30

Open Door policy, 14, 51
Osaka, 80

Peace, conditions for, 62 ff.
Peiping incident of 1937, 11, 32
Peking government, 26
Population problem, 75
Producers' goods, 91, 93

Raw materials, 49, 57, 77, 87, 91
Restoration, 81
Revolution of 1911, 15, 17
Russia, 8, see also U.S.S.R.
Russo-Japanese war, 14, 69, 85

Salt, 57
Samurai, 82
San Min Chu I, 108
Self-determination, 15
Shanghai, 103, 108
  attack by Japan, 30
Social reform, price of, 110
South Manchuria, 28, 29, 30
South Manchuria R.R., 28, 29
Soviet Russia, see U.S.S.R.
Spain, civil war, 73, 113
Sun Yat-sen, 22, 108, 109

Textiles, 47
Third International, 22, 25
Tientsin, 40, 103
Tokugawa Shogunate, 82
Totalitarian blocs, 96
Totalitarianism, 59, 61, 96
Treaty of 1842, 12
Treaty of 1860, 12
Tripartite bloc, 36, 37, 57
Twenty-One Demands, 14

Unequal treaties, 12, 17, 41
U.S.S.R., 6, 9, 88, 89
  aid to China, 33, 71, 72, 93, 112
  and the Far East, 22, 33, 34, 64,
    65, 66
  domination of China, 33, 46
  domination of Far East, 33, 34,
    73
  in North Manchuria, 28
  Kuomintang agreement, 22, 23,
    27
United States, 6, 8, 64
  aid to China, 71, 74
  and a Far East settlement, 65, 66
  economic relations, 48
  Open Door policy, 14, 51
  status quo in Far East, 9

Versailles Treaty, 17, 19

Wang Ching-wei government, 37
Washington Conference, 18-21
West, economic exploitation of Far
    East, 35, 94, 95

West—(*Continued*)
economic reorganization, 95, 96
effect of Chinese victory, 39, 42, 43
  Japanese-controlled China, 58
  Japanese victory, 37, 42, 43
empire relationships, 16
expansion movement, 32
imperialism, 22, 23, 41, 42
industrialization, 33, 46, 76, 81, 87, 107
influence in Japan, 67, 69, 79, 80, 81
special privileges in China, 7, 12, 17, 18, 40, 63

West—(*Continued*)
territorial possessions in Far East, 38
withdrawal from China, 67, 70, 88
  from Far East, 54, 70, 88
  from Japan, 67, 69
Western China, 53
White man's prestige, 16, 40
Wilsonian ideas, 15
World revolution, 22
World War, 33, 34, 45, 69
  effect on China, 14
  effect on Japan, 8, 14

Yangtze Valley, 108